USE LESS STUFF

USE LESS STUFF

Environmental Solutions for Who We Really Are

ROBERT LILIENFELD
DR. WILLIAM RATHJE

USE LESS STUFF

FAWCETT BOOKS
THE BALLANTINE PUBLISHING GROUP
NEW YORK

A Fawcett Book
Published by The Ballantine Publishing Group

http://www.randomhouse.com

Grateful acknowledgment is made to the following for permission to reprint
previously published material:

Chrysalis Music: Excerpt from the lyrics of "Farm on the Freeway" words and
music by Ian Anderson. Copyright © 1987 Chrysalis Music Ltd. All rights in the
U.S. and Canada administered by Chrysalis Music (ASCAP). International
copyright secured. All rights reserved. Used by permission.

Hal Leonard Corp.: Excerpt from the lyrics of "Lord, Mr. Ford" words and
music by Dick Feller. Copyright © 1973 by Sixteen Stars Music and Vector
Music. International copyright secured. All rights reserved.

Maypop Music: Excerpt from the lyrics of "Pass It on Down" by Randy Owen,
Teddy Gentry, Will Robinson, and Ronnie Rogers. Copyright © 1990, Maypop
Music (A Division of Wildcountry, Inc.) (BMI). Used by permission. All rights
reserved.

New Directions Publishing Corporation: Excerpt from "Christ Climbed Down"
from *A Coney Island of the Mind* by Lawrence Ferlinghetti. Copyright © 1958
by Lawrence Ferlinghetti. Reprinted by permission of New Directions
Publishing Corporation.

Library of Congress Cataloging in Publication Data
Lilienfeld, Robert M.
Use less stuff : environmentalism for who we really are /
by Robert M. Lilienfeld, Dr. William L. Rathje.
p.   cm.
ISBN 0-449-00168-7 (alk. paper)
1. Environmentalism.   2. Environmental management.
3. Conservation of natural resources.   4. Recycling (Waste, etc.)
I. Rathje, William L.   II. Title.
GE195.L53   1998
363.7—dc21   98-26903
                                                    CIP

Text design by Ann Gold
Cover design by Barbara Leff

Manufactured in the United States of America

First Edition: November 1998

10 9 8 7 6 5 4 3 2

FOR JOANN, JORDAN, GEOFFREY,
E E, MUKHA, AND KONG-KONG

CONTENTS

CONTENTS

CONTENTS

LIST OF TABLES

INTRODUCTION

Many people have characterized our struggle to take proper care of the environment as a "war on waste."

One poignant "war on waste" story begins on a bitter cold morning in February, when Mr. George Cherson finds himself shivering and nearly frozen stiff as he stands in a long line outside a small train depot in Linden, Massachusetts. A man in his sixties would need a good reason to expose himself to such conditions, and Mr. Cherson has one. It is 1942, just two months after the Japanese sneak attack devastated Pearl Harbor, and Cherson is waiting to register the tires of his Model A Ford and turn in his spares for the war effort. The day before, the War Production Board had announced the rationing of tires (along with iron, steel, tin, aluminum, rags and paper, and animal fat). The WPB decreed that every tire had to be registered by serial number and that each car was to be allowed only one spare; the rest had to be turned in or the culprit would be heavily fined or even sentenced to jail.

Cherson, honest to a fault, is not able to sleep the night of WPB's announcement. He is determined to recycle his spare tires before he does anything else the next morning. However, after several hours waiting outside in bone-chilling weather for bureaucrats inside to process all the forms and details, he is not able to do anything more than return home and collapse. Still, making a personal contribution to smash Tojo and Hitler is well worth enduring the inconvenience and even the cold. That is what Cherson believes and what he often repeats to his family during, and even after, the war years.

Now the story shifts to a train that has carried its passengers out of a New England winter and into the Florida sun. It is the late 1940s, and one of the pilgrims to the south is Mrs. Cherson, an inconspicuous widow who is sitting quietly next to a window and watching the Florida scenery fly past. She becomes interested in the relief from the flat Florida terrain represented by a tall mesa, higher than her line of sight, that stretches out for miles and miles along the tracks as the train speeds south. It takes the lady quite a while to determine the composition of this monstrous unnatural mound, but when she finally does, she breaks into hysterical laughter.

Her astonished companions in the train car try to calm her down. Eventually she is able to blurt out, "Look, out there! There are my husband's tires!" As her son, Peter, later added, "You see, she had tried to dissuade my father from going out that freezing morning—she knew better about government."

The Environmental Protection Agency (EPA), other environmental groups, and the media have assured us time and again that America's finest hour in the "war on waste" occurred during World War II "scrap drives" on the home front. But Mrs. Cherson was right. It turns out that tires weren't the only thing that were collected but never recycled.

Take paper. Suellen Hoy and Michael C. Robinson, in a monograph written for the U.S. Public Works Historical Society, report that the dutiful public's offerings of used wastepaper were so overwhelming that they clogged the paper-collection program almost to constipation. Charitable and public service organizations found themselves with accumulations of wastepaper that weren't valuable enough even to cover their collection costs. More important, the secondary materials dealers, the people who were the bulwark of the physical movement of wastepaper from collection point to recycling facility, found their livelihoods considerably diminished by the wastepaper glut. The result: In order to save the economic viability of professional wastepaper dealers and to keep public disenchantment with wastepaper from spreading to other recyclables, in June 1942 the WPB asked the public to stop saving paper.

What's Going on Here?

The answer is simple: recycling has limits. The leftover tires and paper exemplify a system that couldn't handle the public's response. As a result, many World War II scrap drives were successful mainly as a PR strategy to bolster the morale of those on the home front.

Today, we are faced with a similar situation. We have been asked to do our part to save the environment by recycling, and like those who labored on the World War II home front, we are valiantly doing our best. Our overall recycling rate continues to rise—but so does the amount of trash we discard. We place glass, paper, and plastic into our recycling bins, but much of it sits in bigger piles in warehouses, often with little hope of going anywhere other than a landfill.

To keep recycling from once again becoming little more than a PR effort, we must come to an important realization: recycling by itself cannot solve our environmental degradation/resource conservation/solid-waste dilemma. It is a means to an end, not an end itself. The real end result is the conservation of resources and the minimization of waste. Because it reduces waste that has already been created, recycling can fight only half of the conservation battle. We must begin to fight the other half by implementing a strategy designed to *prevent* waste altogether. That strategy is source reduction, or what we call *using less stuff* (ULS).

In order to make a meaningful contribution to World War II's recycling effort, George Cherson was willing to suffer—and he did! Unfortunately, the results were hardly worth the effort. Today, with this small book about waste prevention (technically known as *source reduction*), you will be able to make a *big* difference *without* suffering.

But first, we need to set the stage a bit by examining our consumption and disposal habits since we left the caves and headed for first the farm and then the city.

LESSONS FROM THE PAST

O Nanna, Ur has been destroyed, its people have been dispersed.
—Anonymous "Lament of the Fall of Ur,"
second millennium B.C.

Q: *What do all the previous civilizations that practiced recycling have in common?*

A: *They're extinct.*

Recycling is not a new phenomenon, as many grandparents and great-grandparents who participated in World War II scrap drives will tell you. But it turns out that the concept has been around much longer than even they realize. From the Sumerians who built the first-ever cities in the Near East 4,000 years ago to modern America, virtually every civilization that has ever existed has tried recycling as a way to save its resources, and ultimately itself, from disappearing.

But it hasn't worked once. Perversely, the reason is not because people didn't try hard enough. The fact is, they tried too hard! By focusing so heavily on recycling and not on the primary reasons that resource availability and environmental problems arose in the first place, societies have consistently missed the real opportunity to sustain natural resources and thus their own human and financial resources.

The Long Tradition of Squandering Resources

As venerated as recycling is in our society today, you may be surprised to learn that not much was recycled until the advent of permanent settlements. In fact, contrary to popular opinion, ancient hunters and gatherers who foraged for plant and animal food for the first 2 million years of human existence do not seem to have worried much about resource conservation if resources were abundant. The sites of hunters' kills, where large game such as mammoth were butchered, are typically littered with tools that were only slightly dulled or damaged. Instead of resharpening the cutting edge to reuse the blade, the butchers would simply whack out a new tool from a fresh piece of stone. The reason is most likely that, as archaeologists who learned to re-create ancient stone tools quickly discovered, resharpening (called "retouching" by archaeologists) takes considerably more effort and skill than making a new tool from scratch.

Conspicuous consumption of resources did not stop at inanimate objects. Animals were often killed and left to rot with an abandon that makes today's trophy hunters look like ardent conservationists. At Prêdmost, Czechoslovakia, about 25,000 years ago, a band of hunters—probably numbering fewer than 300, including their nonhunting dependents—carefully orchestrated a scheme that used fire to drive a herd of horses off a cliff. By identifying the quantity of bone remains that the hunters left behind and studying the articulation of the bones to determine whether their position was natural or the result of movement through butchering, archaeologists found evidence that several hundred were cut up so that meaty parts, such as thighs, could be carried off. They also determined that the bodies of more than 100,000 horses were left behind untouched.

As surprising as it may seem, this massive waste is a common story among ancient hunters. Olsen Chubbuck, a kill site in Colorado that was excavated by the archaeologist Joe Ben Wheat, is another example. Wheat determined that during late May or early June in the year 6500 B.C. or thereabouts, a band of Paleo-Indian hunters stampeded a herd of *Bison occidentalis* (giant bison) into an arroyo. One hundred eighty-five bison were killed. Of these, only thirty-five were completely butchered to extract meaty cuts, twenty more had large limbs removed, the hearts were removed from thirty, another fifty had only their tongues sliced out, and the last fifty were left lying completely intact. In fact, it's been estimated that nearly

70 percent of the large mammals in North America were hunted to extinction by Paleo-Indians.

This pattern of conspicuous consumption and resource squandering is common among hunter-gatherers today where game abounds. In some parts of Australia, for example, Aborigines hunt with shotguns from the backs of speeding pickup trucks. If they bring down a kangaroo, they stop to pick it up. If it is only wounded and hobbles off in a direction other than the way they are headed, they drive on, leaving the kangaroo to die unutilized by those who killed it.

The only real effort at conservation of resources by ancient hunter-gatherers that can be documented by archaeologists occurred when they ventured onto tundra and other open plains where stones suitable for making chipped tools were scarce or nonexistent. In such environments, hunter-gatherers stretched the supply of stones they could carry with them as far as possible by making their tools as small as possible and by constantly resharpening them. Thus, using fewer resources was the primary tactic employed by hunter-gatherers to conserve resources—and the oldest form of garbage minimization!

With the transition to agriculture that started about 10,000 years ago, our ancestors began settling down into permanent villages, towns, and later, cities. This more stationary lifestyle allowed for the collection, storage, and refurbishment of spent items into once-again useful ones. Thus, a new technique was added to humanity's resource conservation arsenal—recycling.

Recycling— Society's Oldest Profession?

Yes, contrary to popular belief, recycling is society's oldest profession. As soon as people stopped moving their camps at frequent intervals and settled down in permanent living quarters, there is archaeological evidence that some residents began specializing in reshaping broken tools into new ones. There are, in fact, clear remains in the archaeological record of workshops where broken or damaged metal was reforged into new tools or weapons; where broken pieces of pottery, called "potsherds" by archaeologists, were ground up and added as "temper" (the material that bonds the clay) in new pots; and even where carved pendants of exotic stones that had broken were recarved into smaller pendants. All these recycling specialties date back long before civilizations first codified laws that formally called attention to people who engaged in unacceptable sexual conduct as a way of making a living.

UR'S RECYCLING AND CONSPICUOUS CONSUMPTION

Four thousand years ago, in what is now the southern reaches of the country of Iraq, the ancient Sumerian city of Ur (the one mentioned in the Old Testament) sat proudly at the center of a vast network of irrigation canals on the banks of the Euphrates River. The good citizens of Ur recycled compulsively. Old metal utensils and weapons, virtually anything made of wood (which was lacking in their palm tree and desert environment), humble pieces of broken pottery, and even grand temples and palaces were turned into new variations of the same.

Implausibly, at the same time they were recycling with obsessive fervor, the residents were degrading their land's future fertility and squandering what wealth they had on public displays of seeming success. In the 1950s, modern-day scholars with the benefit of hindsight discovered that one of the key problems that led to Ur's downfall was self-inflicted. At Ur, the king's bureaucrats instituted agricultural practices that discouraged farmers from their traditional habit of regularly letting their fields lie fallow to decrease salinity and regenerate nutrients in the soil. The rationale for the new agricultural rules was that the government needed food production to keep pace with the burgeoning legions of artisans, merchants, and soldiers, as well as the myriad laborers endlessly toiling on massive temples, palaces, and other monuments of conspicuous consumption being built to memorialize the city's vast hubris. Ur seemed to thrive on using more and more stuff.

Decreased fallow time led to diminished nutrients in the soil and a rise in the water table as a result of constant irrigation. Since irrigation water brought with it large quantities of salts from Iraq's mountains, the soils near the surface became increasingly saline through time. Soon, crop yields in fields with both a high water table and saline soils began to decline sharply.

The bureaucrats, however, did not return to the traditional practice of fallowing fields, which lowered the water table and decreased the salt concentration in the soils. Instead, they encouraged the flagging farmers to plant crops in every field every year. Not content with this measure, they went even farther and pushed the farmers in areas that were still highly productive to plant more often in order to compensate for the overall shortfall. What is obvious to us now—that unrelenting planting and irrigation would lead to salinization that would destroy the land's productivity—was not visible to the bureaucrats of Ur, who kept demanding more from farmers.

At the same time, to keep the farmers' fealty firmly in place, the bureaucracy organized more workers to build even grander public tributes to the city's successes. The last major temple built in Ur covered the area of a football field and reached 80 feet into the air. The whole of the acropolis was festooned with decorative art, and surrounding precincts were chock-full of lavish burials and extravagant offerings to the gods. All this effort required more and more workers, which, in turn, required more and more productivity from lands of diminishing fertility.

The ultimate result, of course, was that the political power of the city-state of Ur collapsed around 2000 B.C. at the hands of warriors from the north who took advantage of Ur's weakened condition. Those people who clung to Ur and its surrounding regions were tragically aware of their past glories. In fact, much of their time was spent lamenting their fate in pathetic rituals accompanied by whining songs that begged the gods to restore their previous riches. The city's sad demise was a disaster that had been to a large degree engineered by its own bureaucrats and that ultimately transformed its agricultural lands into a sparsely populated region traversed today only by nomads, the chance archaeologist, and a few tanks. The contradiction of recycling resources with one hand while conspicuously wasting them with the other seems never to have occurred to the people of Ur.

But Ur was not alone in its folly. Although it was just one petty kingdom of the Ur III and Old Babylonian periods, the rise and fall of Ur mirrored the histories of the polities around it. In fact, the same cycle of the rise and fall of the agricultural base in the region surrounding the Tigris and Euphrates rivers has been repeated again and again. As archaeologist McGuire Gibson concluded, the large catchment drained by these rivers (basically Iraq and a few pieces of surrounding countries) is a land on a "treadmill" because landlords, whether ancient Sumerian kings or Saddam Hussein's henchmen, inevitably opt for quick profits rather than long-term stability.

Through massive irrigation projects that initially increased crop yields but over time promoted waterlogging and salinity, the central governments acted to undermine agricultural productivity. As a result, in the history of the Mesopotamian plain, the damage done to agriculture, and eventually to the plain itself by the central administration, varied according to how strong the government was. To support rapid growth and outrageous displays of economic success, the centralized governments of the Mesopotamian plain shot themselves in their feet.

From four millennia of hindsight, these actions may seem stupid, but they are typical of all the civilizations of our world's history.

THE CLASSIC MAYA, RECYCLING,
AND CONSPICUOUS CONSUMPTION

Half a world away from the ruins of Ur, in the lowland rainforests of the Yucatan Peninsula, the temples and palaces of Classic Maya civilization also lie in ruins.

For more than 500 years, the Classic Maya lived ostentatiously in their jungle home. Over these centuries, the Maya became ever more obsessed with commemorating events in the lives of their rulers and with vicious internecine warfare. No archaeologist has figured out how to measure the resources and energy that went into the fighting. Nevertheless, consider the effort placed into demeaning vanquished enemies and commemorating victories: lavishly sculpted temples on 80-foot-high platforms; richly appointed ball courts; huge stairways covered with glyphic writings; and ritual offerings and elite burials crammed full of stingray spines, decorated bloodred spondylus shells, large pieces of volcanic glass delicately chipped into "eccentric" shapes, and pottery covered with scenes of rulers involved in everything from torturing their enemies to dancing with boa constrictors at the funerals of friends. Clearly, Maya efforts for both war and remembrance were astronomical.

Economically, the Classic Maya flourished by using both slash-and-burn and ridged-field agriculture and by orchestrating a complex network of overland trade routes. Along these, human porters constantly carried handsomely crafted religious geegaws to exchange for mineral salt and other goods that were essential to every Maya household. By the ninth century A.D., the Maya agricultural system was seriously eroded by the need to feed a burgeoning population and the resulting decrease in soil fallow time. Further, the landlocked Classic Maya were abruptly confronted by seafaring merchants from the south coast of the Gulf of Mexico. As a result, Maya cargo carriers had to compete economically against bulk quantities of fancy mold-made pottery and other "mass produced" goods that their competitors transported in large trading canoes.

The mystery of the Maya collapse is that, in the face of impending economic doom, they invested tremendous quantities of resources in the bravado of local warfare and grand temples to honor victories. Such heavy investments, which did nothing to combat the problems of tough economic competition for markets and declining agricultural productivity caused by overplanting to support nonagricultural populations, continued until the very end.

The city of Ur in replay? Yes, but with a vengeance! Since their abrupt abandonment in the ninth century A.D., the Classic Maya cities and their surrounding lands remained unoccupied until the promise of tourism in the twentieth century brought them back to life. It is sadly ironic that when tourists and their dollars were attracted to the Maya's spectacular monuments, the economic payoff came a thousand years too late for the Classic Maya workers who built them.

THE TRAGEDY OF THE
SUMERIANS AND THE CLASSIC MAYA

While today we admire the majesty of Maya and Sumerian temples—even in ruins—it is also easy to see the engineered disasters that befell the local populations. Both civilizations—the Sumerian and the Classic Maya—recycled with gusto. They literally turned old buildings into new. The Sumerians flattened derelict structures to serve as foundations for new structures that were much higher. Sumerian holy words often supported religious observances literally, since broken clay tablets covered with religious texts were regularly used as foundation fill for temples and other structures. When it came to either temples or palaces, the Maya didn't raze a building that was being replaced. Instead, they just added a thick outer shell on top, thereby guaranteeing that the latest temple or palace would be bigger than its predecessors.

Both civilizations also recycled daily utensils and tools. The Sumerians had metallurgy and collected and reforged swords, plowshares, and pruning hooks. The Maya often worked broken or chipped stone tools into new shapes that had different uses.

The Maya shared an exquisite irony with the Sumerians before them. All of these ardent recyclers, who reused and recycled tools down to nubbins, never seemed to see the inconsistency in placing hundreds, or even thousands, of totally unused tools in caches to dedicate a building or in the ritual interment of the community's elite. Clearly, both recycling and conspicuous consumption were taken as facts of life that were not to be challenged. Perhaps, in fact, when it came to resource management and conservation, the forest of conspicuous consumption could not be seen through all the twigs and branches of the trees of recycling.

Have We Learned from the Lessons of the Past?

Few expressions are more familiar or widely accepted than "Those who don't learn from the past are doomed to repeat it." In fact, our society has spent more time and effort than any other on the face of the earth in studying past societies in order to learn about the problems they faced and the missteps they made that led to their downfall.

So what have we learned from all this history that can help us avoid a similar fate? Not that much, we're afraid. Here we are, thousands of years later, passionately recycling, yet consuming with equal gusto!

Once again, we stand on the precipice, poised to make great technological and economic strides, while potentially destroying the environment on which, and from which, all our successes have been built. A look at the potential environmental catastrophes we face can show us why, if we don't stop and rethink our priorities and strategies, the same results might ultimately befall our descendants.

A handful of major issues have been singled out by scientists, environmentalists, policy planners, and the general public as the most serious environmental problems we currently face. These are the problems that seem most likely to lead to a significant degradation, or even collapse, of our late-twentieth-century lifestyles of comfort and convenience, thanks to unwelcome and possibly unforeseen changes in global ecosystems. They are as follows:

- Overpopulation
- Global warming
- Ozone depletion
- Habitat destruction
- Loss of biodiversity
- Depletion of nonrenewable natural resources
- Increased pollution and waste generation

These are huge problems compared to those faced in past societies. What's more, these problems are global, rather than regional or local. Thus, unlike our hunting and gathering ancestors and their nomadic offspring, there's nowhere left for us to run, since geographically speaking, we're already there!

While all these issues are the focus of concern, their current status and the rate of environmental degradation caused by them are the source of major debates. For example, few people would dispute that the effects of global warming would be catastrophic: both the East and West coasts of the United States would disappear under a flood of water released from melting polar caps, and weather patterns would change, with fertile plains becoming deserts, and deserts fertile plains. Yet many business leaders don't feel there's enough information available to indicate that global warming is occurring, leading them to promote the status quo. The problem with this strategy is—and a few progressive business leaders will admit to this point—if we wait to make sure that the problem exists, when we are finally certain that it does, it will be far too late to do anything to stop it.

Frankly, we find this status quo attitude on the part of modern business leaders to be somewhat surprising, given the current penchant for reengineering and quality management. It's even more confounding when one assesses the situation by applying risk analysis, a favorite quantitative tool in the world of commerce.

Risk analysis looks at two major factors: a.) the degree of risk, and b.) its size or magnitude. A situation with a high degree of risk and a high level of magnitude is obviously a major concern. A situation with a low level of risk and a low magnitude is just the opposite, and a problem with high risk and low magnitude also falls in this "not to worry" category.

It's the last of the four possible scenarios that concerns us: low risk and high magnitude. Most businesspeople tend to shrug off huge environmental concerns because they feel that the risk is low or that it has not yet been demonstrated to be high enough in their minds to warrant attention. And therein lies the problem: *many of the issues we're talking about are so huge that even a small level of probability should be enough to cause careful thought as well as corrective action.*

In situations involving a whole series of potentially severe problems enmeshed in mountains of debate and disagreement, it would seem logical to find an equal diversity in the number of promoted solutions. Ironically, there is little or no debate over the solution to environmental woes. Virtually everyone's first action of choice is—recycling. Is the recycling response aimed at the target's bull's-eye? Unfortunately, the answer is no. To understand why, we have to take a hard look at what recycling can and cannot do, within the context of solving our large global issues.

First, overpopulation. Obviously, no amount of recycling (except for possibly turning latex gloves into condoms) is going to slow the population growth rate. (Too bad we can't take to population control the way we've taken to recycling! Even China, once known for its stringent one-child-per-couple policy, is permitting couples the luxury of a second child.)

What about global warming? Again, with a few hardly significant exceptions, the answer has to be no. The reason is that global warming is caused by one of the things we are not capable of recycling: energy. In fact, recycling may actually contribute to the increase in greenhouse gases and to a decrease in the supply of nonrenewable resources.

You're probably asking yourself, *how is this possible?* Like virtually everything else, recycling involves many processes—collection, transportation, cleaning, manufacture, storage, transport again, and sale—that use energy and generate pollutants just like manufacturing from virgin materials does. The most common denominator, of course, is the gasoline required to move goods around. This is true even when comparing initial procurement of virgin materials with procurement of recyclables, since collecting recyclables means that garbage company trucks now run their routes twice—once for discards and once for recyclables. Thus, the combination of using up nonrenewable resources and the damage caused by pollution can far outweigh the benefits of collecting, reprocessing, and transporting recyclables.

How about ozone depletion? Since it's widely accepted that the ozone hole was largely related to the use of CFCs and similar chemical compounds, recycling isn't going to change the picture. In fact, the recycling of CFCs will just produce a continued slow drain into the atmosphere. The best thing to do is what the Montreal Protocol set out to do: replace theses substances with effective, but environmentally benign, substitutes.

What about habitat destruction, loss of biodiversity, and depletion of nonrenewable resources? Recycling can make a difference, but in the long term it will not be enough. This is due to the fact that recycling merely delays the impacts of consumption; it does not decrease them. Recycling does, of course, expand the "use-life" of resources; but eventually they fall out of the recycle-production-consumption cycle, either because they are thrown into the garbage by mistake or carelessness or, more likely, because they degrade after being recycled and cannot be recycled again.

Paper, for example, can be recycled, on average, only three times before its fibers are too short and the ink residue too dense to continue to produce a functional recycled product. Recycling will keep each tree's fiber circulating longer; nevertheless, if consumption of paper products continues to increase (and there's no reason to think otherwise), the impact on the environment of cutting trees will also increase. More paper will be recycled, but more paper will also eventually drop out of the system, and more wood fiber will be procured. Thus, recycling will not stop or even simply diminish the various impacts on the environment created by consumption that aggravate global warming (such as emissions from gasoline burned in transportation), or ozone depletion (such as the release of volatile organic compounds [VOCs] in solvents used in industrial cleaning processes), or habitat destruction and loss of biodiversity (such as procuring resources or building new facilities).

OK, but what about increased pollution and waste generation? Recycling must have zeroed in on these problems, and pollution and waste generation are surely decreasing! While it's true that pollution has declined significantly, the changes have far more to do with successful pollution prevention than with recycling. (And as we just stated above, recycling pollutes as well.)

Sadly, the supposition of reduced waste generation is also highly debatable. It is true, of course, that about 27 percent of the materials that would have been discarded are now collected separately for recycling. At the same time, however, we are throwing more and more nonrecyclables away. This is due to a perverse behavior pattern called "Parkinson's Law of Garbage." A derivative of Parkinson's Law, it states: *Garbage will expand to fill the space provided for it.*

Today, many communities have switched to automated garbage collection systems that require standard-size cans of a large size—usually 90-gallon drums. In place of the old standard galvanized-steel 40-gallon cans, the 90-gallon garbage mausoleums provide plenty of space for what was once destined for attics, basements, or storage sheds—such as many items that are considered "household hazardous wastes" (unused paints and pesticides, for example), used materials that might once have been donated to a charitable organization (old clothes, furniture, appliances, and so on), yard wastes that might otherwise have been composted, and even recyclables that might otherwise have been recycled.

The harsh reality is that regardless of recycling rates, we continue to dump at least as much as we have ever dumped—over 160 million tons annually; global warming continues to be a major threat, thanks to the continued production of huge amounts of carbon dioxide, nitrates, and sulfates; the ozone hole may not still be growing, but even so, it will not be back to its pre-1980 self for another hundred years or so; and "urban flight," combined with our constant creation of, and migration to, the artificially "natural" environments of suburbs, continues to destroy millions of acres of wildlife habitat.

All of this means that, like the residents of Ur and the Classic Maya before us, we have not matched our solutions to the most important problems we currently face.

Lessons for Us Today

One of the most significant conclusions of archaeology, validated by being taken together with a review of our current environmental status, is that all civilizations—from the earliest to us today—have primarily used recycling as a means to conserve resources and thus cope with their resource management woes and wastes. The disturbing fact is that all earlier civilizations now lie in ruins, and it seems certain that if we follow the path we are on without modification, our remains will soon lie beside them. As a result, it would seem prudent for us to examine two questions raised by the trajectories of ancient societies and our contemporary plight:

1. *Why, at the same time we are recycling, do we feel the need to define success by wasting resources?* This is really not such a difficult question to answer. The behavior of recycling and wasting at the same time is not logical, but it is all too human. We all do it. Have you ever driven miles to a recycling center in a gas-guzzling car to turn in a few cents' worth of newspapers? Or, how about discarding 5 pounds of mail-order catalogs on the same day you place 3 pounds of materials out by the curb in your recycling bin? When we do things like this as individuals, it seems understandable. When we do such things as whole societies, it seems crazy—but still all too human.

2. *Why has recycling been the conservation method of choice throughout history?* The most obvious reason is that people did not see the big picture clearly enough to determine where the most critical threat lay. Thus, the government of Ur did not comprehend their environmental degradation and resource waste problems and consequently followed policies that not only did not cure the difficulties but served to exacerbate them. The Classic Maya, as well, seem not only to have missed seeing the need to compete in trade by investing manpower and resources into new techniques and product designs, but also invested their available manpower and other resources primarily in nonproductive forms of warfare and conspicuous consumption.

Similarly today, we recycle with gusto as we discard 20 million tons of food a year, offer "no annual fee" credit cards to teenagers, and barrage homeowners to remortgage their houses in order to consume more things that will eventually become waste. Thus, although separated by vast gulfs of time and geography, each of these societies didn't—or don't—see their most pressing problems, concentrating instead on recycling and material displays of success—an illogical but familiar human foible.

So, finally, what *is* the real issue we must face?

It's Consumption, Pure and Simple!

The simple truth is that *all* of our major environmental concerns are either caused by, or contribute to, the ever-increasing consumption of goods and services. But rather than deal with the effects of too much shopping and purchasing, we've taken the time-honored path of shooting the messengers—the packaging, dirty disposable diapers, foam cups, and other discards that are signs of consumption but are not really consumption itself. And in so doing, we have focused only on the symptoms—too much waste and pollution—and not the underlying problem itself.

In this context, recycling is merely an aspirin, alleviating a rather large collective hangover. But just as aspirin does not prevent hangovers, recycling will not prevent overconsumption. In fact, by putting too much faith in recycling, we are actually rewarding ourselves for over-consuming. Think about it. We feel good when we fill the recycling bin. In reality, we should feel good when there's no waste to put in it at all!

What can we do to stop ourselves from becoming the next Sumerians or classic Mayas? Maybe if we examine the common mistakes we all make as humans in a new light, we can find clues to creating workable solutions.

HOW DID WE GET LIKE THIS?

To a person with a hammer, all problems look like a nail.
—Japanese proverb

Why do we humans always seem to shoot ourselves in the collective foot? Are we stupid? Unwilling or unable to learn from history and our past mistakes? Is it really true that the road to hell is paved with good intentions?

To answer these questions, we must step back and take a long and pragmatic look at ourselves. We know from a wide variety of scientific studies that *Homo sapiens* is a highly social species that initially organized into small groups of hunter-gatherers. Humans continued living in this fairly nomadic condition for at least 2 million years.

It has been less than 10,000 years since we started congregating in towns, cities, and nations; discovered agriculture; codified laws; and developed commerce, literature, and fine arts. While this seems like a long time based upon our personal perspectives, it is absolutely meaningless from an evolutionary standpoint—merely 500 generations. This is not nearly enough time for us to have genetically evolved even a tiny bit from the hunter-gatherer societies created and continually reinforced by our first human ancestors over more than *100,000* generations!

Because we have only recently developed complex societies and cultures, we are still genetically programmed to think and act exactly as our ancestors did. Thus, we are literally not equipped with the mental hardware and software required to deal with the modern environments we have created, but instead are programmed to react as if we still lived a million years ago. As a result, we have become modern-day urban sophisticates who are blessed with a previously unknown level of comfort and safety, but who respond to threats and other situations as if we were still living in unforgiving environments. The same is true of the ways in which we take care of our families. The only difference between the hunter running through the bush who brings home the bison and the salesperson running for the plane who brings home the bacon is the form of transportation, choice of clothing, and weapons used to make the kill.

Next time you're standing in front of a window, look outside and make a mental note of the first thing you see. Odds are, it will be something that's moving, like a car, rather than something that's stationary, like a tree. We're programmed to notice movement because a million years ago the ability to recognize and react to things that moved may have meant the difference between life and death—

either by avoiding dangerous situations or finding and trapping the family's next meal.

Even when we're not actively scanning our environment, we are genetically prepared to react to potentially dangerous situations. For example, loud noises cause us to stop what we're doing and focus on the sound so that we can determine if a reaction is necessary. This mechanism is known as the *orienting reflex* and is at the mild end of the various involuntary reflexes designed to ensure survival by escalating our responses to potential dangers. These responses range from simple awareness all the way to the "superhuman" strength available to us in dire emergencies when, with no conscious effort or mental self-discussion, our brains order huge amounts of adrenaline to be released into our bloodstreams.

Deep down, then, we have been designed by the pressures of evolution to take quick and decisive action, as this was the best way to ensure survival in the hostile environments in which we initially found ourselves. The same type of "fight or flight" thinking has caused us to embrace expedient, simple solutions when faced with the highly complex problems and crises of today.

If we are to start making better decisions for the future, we must first understand the mental marching orders that we carry with us from the past. In so doing, we will better understand why we react the way we do and can take appropriate steps to avoid well-intentioned, but potentially costly and ineffective, actions.

It turns out that many, if not most, of our conclusion-drawing and decision-making processes are designed right into our nervous systems. Some of these automatic routines are apparently built into our most basic genetic instruction sets (akin to computer firmware, or ROM), while others are more like mental software that automatically boots itself up whenever our brains think it is needed.

There is an entire field devoted to the study of the mental tricks we use to help make decisions. It's called *heuristics*, and it analyzes the little rules of thumb that seem to be hardwired into our heads. While these biases may have been lifesaving when we wandered the savanna and the plains, they may actually be life threatening now that we have settled down to live in places like Savannah, Georgia, and Des Plaines, Illinois.

Here are but a few of the many ways in which we are programmed to think and act, with an emphasis on those heuristics, or rules of thumb, we use when relating to issues concerning the environment:

We tend to see issues in black-and-white.

We humans like our decisions to be simple—either yes or no. Shades of gray tend to make us uncomfortable because they signal that an issue will be complex, might have more than one solution, and will require a frustratingly long time to resolve. We far prefer issues that can be seen in black-and-white terms.

It seems that we can't help but think this way, as we've been doing so since time immemorial. A group of anthropologists discovered that the uses of color, and the terms associated with it, differ markedly among cultures. Some societies have names for only a few colors, while others are able to describe hundreds. A rank ordering of color awareness and social complexity turned up something rather amazing: as cultural complexity increases, the number of color terms increases as well. In the United States, *The New Student Color Set* lists more than 500 colors used every day in our society. In contast, the most primitive hunting and gathering cultures in existence today use only two terms when discussing color: light and dark!

What is important is that people in less technologically advanced societies are not physiologically different from those of us in more sophisticated societies. They are perfectly capable of seeing as many colors as we do. Given their more basic everyday concerns, needs, and consumption habits, they simply have no reason to do so.

Thus, it appears that while we have learned to recognize and describe many colors, tones, and hues, our most basic tendency is to perceive and describe only two: black and white. These two opposing shades are even used to help identify and illustrate moral concepts such as right and wrong. In Western thinking, for example, white stands for purity, truth, and happiness; black represents evil, fear, and grief. (Anyone who goes to see an old cowboy film can immediately tell the good guys from the bad guys by the color of their hats.)

This type of "either/or" thinking is a primary reason that we place so much emphasis on recycling. We have come to believe that doing it is "good" and not doing it is "bad." Sadly, we have even made the very young feel as if the only morally responsible way to save resources is through recycling. This point was driven home to us while hosting an environmental event at, of all places, the Mall of America. Standing in front of a number of food items, we asked children to tell us what they did with the packages once the food was eaten. When we would point to an item that would obviously go into the trash can, such as a candy wrapper, children would look guiltily at their parents and then at us. With grim smiles laced with uncertainty and hesitation, many answered rhetorically: "We recycle it?"

We confront issues only when they come to a boil, ignoring the causes and dealing instead with the effects.

"Out of sight, out of mind" is more than an expression, it is a statement of fact. We are not very good at anticipating or preventing problems, but prefer to wait for them to happen and then try to remedy the results. We'd rather deal with issues on an after-the-fact basis, trying to reduce the effects of our actions instead of working to eliminate the underlying causes.

Our propensity to "remedy" and "mitigate," rather than to "prevent" and "moderate," can be seen in many important daily issues. We look for the next fad diet, no-fat snack, or weight-loss pill instead of eating properly and exercising. We take hangover cures instead of drinking moderately. We clamor for morning-after pills and quick divorces rather than use birth control or go for counseling. And we try to reduce waste primarily by recycling our newspapers and packaging, instead of recognizing that the products that come in those packages consume about twenty times more resources than do the packages themselves.

The opposite side of our "sky is falling" mental wiring is the fact that once we realize that a specific danger has passed or been overstated, we tend to drop the issue and go back to what we were doing. In the waste generation area, an overstatement alluding to environmental catastrophe could easily lead to our removing the topic from our collective consciousness rather than adjust our vision to deal with the apparently less urgent, but still important, reality of many environmental issues. Paradoxically, this starts the "out of sight, out of mind" process all over again.

We are most concerned with issues when they are close to us in terms of time, space, and personal relationships.
We are not good at reacting to problems that will occur far in the future, are not in our own neighborhoods, or don't directly affect ourselves or our families. It's as if we have mental radar screens and are focused only on those blips that represent immediate danger to us.

You may be relieved to note that there is a firm biological basis for this behavior. Evolutionary biologists such as Richard Dawkins believe that our bodies are basically vessels for our genes and vehicles by which these selfish bits of DNA continue to exist. Our primary purpose, then, is to reproduce successfully so that our genes can propel themselves into the future through our offspring.

To reproduce successfully, we obviously must live long

enough to make it through adolescence, find a mate, have offspring, and raise our children so that they, too, can survive and reproduce. Two strategies we use to increase the odds of success include (1) not taking risks that might reduce our chances of reproduction, and (2) reacting defensively to protect ourselves and those genetically closest to us—our children and siblings. In fact, studies of kin selection clearly indicate that the odds of our putting ourselves in harm's way for others is directly related to the percentage of genetic material we share with them—the higher the percentage, the more likely we are to help. So what looks like altruism is more likely a form of genetic selfishness!

This "selfish gene" factor helps explain why we have such a hard time understanding and dealing with an issue like global warming. It may be vast, but it is not going to happen in the foreseeable future. The "selfish gene" factor is also the reason for the NIMBY (Not In My Back Yard) effect: It's OK to site a landfill or incinerator anywhere, as long as it doesn't affect me or my family.

And of course this factor explains why we have taken to recycling. Having the local landfill overflow and shut down has a direct impact on us, in the sense that there will no longer be any place to put *our* garbage. Thus, recycling helps to solve a problem that seems more immediate and personally relevant than the truly big environmental issues of our time.

We see only what we want to see.
This bias is known as *selective perception*. It means that we interpret data to fit the perception we already have

or the conclusion we've already drawn. When it comes to recycling, selective perception helps us magnify positive news so that our preconceived notions are confirmed and reinforced. Unfortunately, it also allows us to filter out those signals that indicate we may be asking more of recycling than it can possibly achieve.

We are all very confident in our own judgments.

We think we know things we really don't know and refuse to believe we're wrong, even in the face of overwhelming evidence. Research has shown that even when confronted with irrefutable evidence that their position is wrong, people cling tenaciously to their beliefs. (It took the Catholic church hundreds of years to admit that the Sun, and not Earth, is the center of the solar system—and to pardon Galileo for saying so.) When living in small bands or tribes, this approach may have been a very useful way to maintain one's status or self-esteem, but it can be very detrimental in a technological society where seemingly small errors in decision making may ultimately have staggering consequences for immense numbers of people.

Recycling suffers from this situation as well. Solid-waste experts will be among the first to admit that recycling is important, but it is not the primary way to ensure clean air and water or continued biodiversity, or to minimize the chances of global warming or continued destruction of the ozone layer. Yet society as a whole continues to believe that recycling will "save" the planet. This belief is constantly reinforced by governments, environmental groups, educators, and those trade associations that wrap themselves in the recycling mantle in order to appear "green."

The problem is that even as we recycle more and more, we also continue to increase the amount being thrown away. As shown in table 2.1, the recycling rate has grown from 7 percent in 1960 to about 27 percent today, with the amount of solid waste recycled annually having jumped from 6 million to 56 million tons. But the amount of stuff we don't recycle has jumped as well—from 82 million to 152 million tons of trash.

TABLE 2.1

MUNICIPAL SOLID WASTE IN THE UNITED STATES

	1960		1995	
	MM TONS	%	MM TONS	%
Total waste generated	88	100	209	100
Waste recycled	6	7	56	27
Net discards	82	93	152	73

Source: U.S. Environmental Protection Agency.

There is an important lesson hidden in the table that we call the percentage paradox: *a higher recycling percentage does not necessarily mean less overall waste*. The reason is that we recycle pounds, not percentages. Remember, we recycled 27 percent of municipal solid waste (MSW) in 1995 versus 7 percent in 1960. Nevertheless, in 1995 we dumped 70 million more tons of MSW into landfills than we did in 1960. Yet environmentalists, trade associations, the government, and the media mention only the percentages, which are generally holding steady or increasing. This approach tends to paint a comfortable picture, since we feel better when we hear that recycling percentages are rising.

Unfortunately, this has lulled us into a false sense of security because garbage discards—the trash that ends up in landfills—have grown 40 percent faster than garbage that is "diverted" via municipal and commercial recycling programs. Thus, for every extra pound of materials we recycle, we send an additional 1.4 pounds to landfills.

Here is a way to put all of this in perspective: If garbage is an iceberg, the part we recycle is merely the tip—the part above the waterline. The far bigger part rests below, where we can't see it. As we all know, ignoring what we can't or don't want to see can be the biggest danger of all.

We look for ways to maintain the status quo.

Oh, how we hate change! In fact, anthropologists categorize a society by its ability to create and accept change. There is an entire field devoted to the way in which new ideas and innovations diffuse and are accepted by societies, with wide-ranging lessons for any organization trying to influence the public's opinions or behaviors.

Social research, along with a relatively new branch of mathematics called *game theory*, have both shown that we strongly resist losing what we have, and that the more we have to lose, the less likely we are to change. This is a critical reason for our strong recycling ethic: recycling allows us to keep consuming as much as we want to, since it deals only with our disposal habits, not our purchase behavior. In a perverse way, recycling rewards us for consuming: the more stuff we put in the recycling bin, the better we feel. In reality, we should be trying to minimize the amount of stuff we need to recycle by conserving resources in the first place!

The good news is that game theory also predicts that the more we have to gain, the more likely we are to change. In chapter 4, we begin discussing how we might magnify this ray of hope. But first, we need to explore the key social and technological reasons for our seeming lack of interest in conservation and sound environmental decision making.

ADDING NURTURE TO NATURE

They say they gave me compensation.
That's not what I'm chasing, I was a rich man before yesterday.
Now all I have left is a broken down pickup truck.
Looks like my farm is a freeway.
—Jethro Tull, "Farm on the Freeway"

Discussions of human behavior inevitably wind down to the issue of nature versus nurture: are the actions that occur the result of our genes or our environment? When it comes to understanding why and how we consume resources, the answer turns out to be both. The foibles of human nature discussed in the last chapter account for only half the reasons why we should be so concerned about our role in environmental degradation. As we now discuss, our social and cultural traits have led to significant ecological destruction as well.

Understanding why and how human cultures affect the

earth's ecosystems is of critical importance, as the environmental cost of maintaining human societies has been accelerating. The past 200 years of our existence have produced a level of destruction and extinction not seen since the dinosaurs disappeared about 65 million years ago. In fact, some evolutionary biologists have nicknamed our current situation "The Sixth Extinction," to point out that the rate at which species are currently disappearing is as great and potentially cataclysmic as the five major extinction waves known to have previously occurred (without human intervention).

Ironically, a number of our most severe environmental problems are related to many of the activities, trends, and technologies that have significantly increased our quality of life and standard of living over the last century. Thus, as we have bettered our personal environments, we have inadvertently degraded our natural ones. Since we are a part of the ecosystems we are destroying, our current path can only lead us toward a reduction in the quality of life we have come both to enjoy and to expect.

Further adding fuel to the fire is the fact that many of the technologies and activities that negatively affect the environment are interrelated, creating what we call *negative synergy*. Negative synergy occurs when deep interrelationships between variables cause more environmental damage than would result if the key factors occurred but were not related. This situation leads to processes that are nonlinear in scope, meaning that outcomes are not merely arithmetic but geometric.

For example, let's assume that three gases—carbon

dioxide, water vapor, and methane—account for the majority of the greenhouse affect. Let's also assume that if any one of these gases increases by some known factor, the amount of additional heat trapped in the atmosphere increases by 5 percent. (Remember, this is a hypothetical example!) But what happens if two of the gases increase by this factor? A linear, arithmetical relationship would predict an increase in warming of up to 10 percent, since $5 + 5 = 10$. However, a nonlinear, geometrical relationship would predict an increase of up to 25 percent, since $5 \times 5 = 25$.

It is significant to note that as the numbers increase in magnitude, so too does the disparity between the arithmetical and geometrical answers. Geometric effects, such as those used in this hypothetical example, are indicative of large complex systems. Solving these types of problems thus requires taking a more strategic and systems-oriented approach, instead of looking for a simple or superficial answer.

What are the factors that have led to today's environmental problems? Let's discuss the major ones from a historical perspective so that their interrelationships within large systems—our interdependent metroplexes and the local, regional, and national cultures they embody—become apparent.

Advances in Sanitation and Immunization

Since 1900, the world population has more than tripled, growing from 1.6 billion to about 5.9 billion people today.

The reasons for this increase lie in the fact that (1) average global life expectancy rose from 30 to 64 years, and (2) we have experienced significant reductions in global infant mortality—from 170 deaths per 1,000 births in 1950 to fewer than 60 today. Nicholas Eberstadt, a Visiting Fellow at Harvard University's Center for Population Studies, summed it up best when he said, *"Rapid population growth has occurred not because human beings started breeding like rabbits but because they finally stopped dropping like flies."*

This large population gain affects the environment in many ways, the primary one being that people are re-source consumers, rather than producers. We may conserve some forests as parklands, but we do not produce new ones or "bank" old ones except in order to use them in the future. Clearly, we consider all of the earth's bounty to be ours to exploit—and no country has had more re-sources to exploit or has done it faster or with more gusto than the United States.

Modern, affluent societies require vast amounts of materials, energy, and space. And thanks to the second law of thermodynamics, which loosely states that all activities produce waste as they turn order into disorder, there's no free lunch: production and consumption of resources generate "disorder" in the form of pollution, greenhouse gases, and plain old everyday trash. Thus, regardless of one's stance on population growth and control, it is hard to deny that a large global population growing in affluence, even if not in size, represents a significant threat to regional habitats and ecosystems, as well as to the biosphere itself.

As an example, consider the fact that the population growth rate in the United States is virtually flat, at about 1 percent annually. The problem is that this small increase is applied against a large population base—270 million people, in this case. The result is a big one: Our nation's population grows by 2.7 million individuals annually, enough to create a city the size of St. Louis each and every year. At about 1.5 billion people, a similar growth rate in China would produce six times this effect, in the form of 15 million new faces who must be fed, clothed, and housed annually.

What were the causes of enormous gains in life expectancy and population? A primary factor was the realization that diseases such as cholera and diphtheria were caused by germs and that the odds of coming into contact with germs could be reduced. The mid-nineteenth-century efforts of scientists such as Louis Pasteur and Joseph Lister led to the pasteurization of milk and the sterilization of wounds and hospital operating rooms. Along with the chlorination of drinking water and the advent of sanitary sewers and indoor plumbing, these discoveries rank among the most important lifesaving measures of all time.

A second critical (and interrelated) life-extending factor was the discovery of vaccines and antibiotics that could immunize against, or mitigate the effects of, such deadly or crippling diseases as whooping cough, measles, smallpox, and polio. Even afflictions that are considered minor, or are easily treated today, were killers only a few generations ago. For example, until laboratory synthesis of penicillin in 1957, families routinely lost children to common ear infections. (One of the authors lost two great aunts to ear infections, and would have lost his mother to this disease as well, if not for then newly available antibiotics.) And polio, which is virtually unheard of today, was a killing and crippling childhood disease up until the early 1960s, when an oral vaccine developed by Jonas Salk was widely, and often freely, distributed. (A close cousin of the other author carries the scars of polio, and both authors remember the palpable fear this disease engendered in their parents and relatives. They also remember swallowing that grape-flavored vaccine, alongside their classmates, in their grade-school gyms.)

The Automobile

No invention has done more to extend Americans' self-image as freewheeling, frontier-frolicking, and fun-loving folks than the automobile. Without it, there would be no highways, suburbs, or shopping malls. Vast portions of the economy would not exist, either. There would be no car companies or dealers, tire companies, oil companies, gas stations, auto parts suppliers and retailers, car washes, or a whole truckload of other related businesses.

But with the good comes the bad. Every second in

America, cars collectively burn 3,000 gallons of gasoline and release 60,000 pounds of carbon dioxide into the atmosphere. In fact, automobiles consume about one-third of the energy used in the United States and create about two-thirds of its carbon dioxide emissions, produce 90 percent of the carbon monoxide found in urban air, and are responsible for about half of all atmospheric pollution.

As cars guzzle gas and spew pollution, their presence shapes our environment in other ways as well. Almost 40 million acres of American soil have been turned into roads and parking lots. We throw away 200 million tires annually. At least 170 million of the 300 million gallons of the motor oil used each year are disposed of improperly. For reference, a gallon of used oil can contaminate a million gallons of groundwater.

What's more, the rest of the world can't wait to catch up! This situation presents the potential for huge increases in greenhouse gas emissions and other pollutants, not to mention fossil fuel use. For example, China and India contain about 40 percent of the world's population. If both nations eventually allowed for the same number of cars per person as exists in the United States today (about 0.6 cars per person), the total number of cars and the resulting fuel use and pollution would increase by a factor of nine. There would be nearly a billion cars in China alone—and we think congestion and pollution are debilitating in New York and Los Angeles!

This type of automobile-related development leads to the creation of huge metroplexes. For example, about 40 percent of the entire population of Mexico lives in Mexico City. The environmental woes suffered by all living creatures in and around this megametropolis are both legion and well known.

Suburbs and the Roads That Reached Them

World War II brought a new fear to politicians and the American public: the threat of a German attack on the industrial machine that was winning the war effort. With most plants concentrated in the East and Midwest, the federal government began building facilities in harder-to-reach areas where land was cheap: the South, Southwest, and West. Cities such as Los Angeles, New Orleans, San Diego, Portland, and Houston saw their populations and economies mushroom. So, too, did their metropolitan regions.

Combined with this nationwide expansion was a local expansion in the form of "suburbification." In 1944, the GI Bill of Rights led to guarantees that 16 million veterans would be able to purchase homes. Within two years, housing starts multiplied eightfold. Since city lands were both expensive and chock-full, nearby farms, woodlands, and marshes began to disappear, along with the animals, insects, fungi, and bacteria dependent upon these ecosystems and their plants for existence.

The year 1944 also saw the passage of the Federal-Aid Highway Act, which created the National Interstate Highway System. Building the interstates required movement of enough dirt to add two feet of topsoil to the entire state of Connecticut—and the laying of enough concrete to pave the state of Delaware completely. Running these smooth, wide roads through the heartland and right into our cities destroyed key parts of both—small towns became backwaters, and cities lost many of their oldest and most diverse neighborhoods. The flight to the suburbs was only exacerbated by these factors, as well as by the increased congestion and pollution in metropolitan areas.

Today, with the service economy's educated and affluent workers looking to live and work in clean, safe environments, both they and their employers continue to leave the inner cities, moving to nearby suburbs and turning them into "edge cities" or cities at the periphery of cities—giant complexes combining shopping centers, office parks, and housing developments. Wetlands, farms, and fields continue to be gobbled up by these fast-growing mini-metropolises near cities such as New York, Atlanta, San Francisco, and Detroit. With these edge cities easily accessible by major highways, the once-rural fringes that used to be considered too far from downtown for commuting are quickly becoming the new suburbs and bedroom communities of tomorrow.

Mass Marketing and Communication

In the early part of the twentieth century, shopping was an everyday affair. People purchased food and other staples from different outlets: butcher shops, produce stands, and general stores. Milk and other dairy products were delivered to customers' doors by the farmers themselves. Stores offered what today would be considered very high levels of service, with shopkeepers doing the picking, extending credit, and making deliveries.

In 1912, this all started to change. In the East, the Great Atlantic & Pacific Tea Company, now known as A&P, began experimenting with economy stores that offered lower prices. The shops provided neither credit nor deliveries, hence the reason for their being known as cash-and-carry stores. In the West and South, retailers began tinkering with another new cost-saving wrinkle: self-service.

Three factors came together to give these fledgling concepts a major jump start. First, the number of automobile registrations between 1920 and 1930 soared, from 8 million to 23 million. America was now far more mobile, moving between farm, city, and suburb. Customers could travel easily to the new stores, and suppliers could make deliveries to them as well.

Second, at the tail end of this automotive boom came the Great Depression. To help Americans cope with their reduced financial circumstances, the first true supermarket opened in New York in 1930. The King Kullen chain proudly announced its ability to cut costs by boldly advertising itself as "The World's Greatest Price Wrecker." The cost of getting food and other staples to consumers continued to decline. Chains that had both the most and the biggest stores developed the greatest economies of scale and eventually came to dominate the marketplace. Today there are more than 150,000 grocery stores and supermarkets in the United States, with sales of $425 billion. Almost 3.5 million people are employed by these stores. With their rows and rows of shelves, stores are able to stock both more of an item and more items. (The average number of products in a supermarket currently stands at 30,000.)

Third, the advent of first radio and then television opened up entirely new ways to deliver news and entertainment to the vast majority of Americans. The costs of programming, production, and transmission were borne by advertisers, who paid for the right to deliver sales messages to audiences that were far bigger and far more efficient to reach than with traditional media, such as newspapers or magazines. These mass communications created an enormous feedback loop that helped fill the coffers of radio and television networks and, likewise, of car companies, supermarket chains, and other advertisers. By reaching millions upon millions of people with their messages, consumer goods companies were able to generate high levels of demand, which allowed them to build large economies of scale, which lowered unit costs and thus created additional demand.

Adding to the positive feedback was the fact that sales of consumer goods were becoming more efficient and centralized, thanks to the newly created supermarket chains and their strengthened purchasing power and efficient buying and distribution systems. Everyone profited: consumers received lower prices, while stores, advertisers, and media companies received higher profits.

Other types of retailers took note of these innovations, changing the face of nonfood retailing and distribution as well. Shopping malls sprang up in fields and pastures, where land was cheap and parking was ample. Seeing increased dollars from sales taxes in their future, state and county managers built roads to carry people to and from these centers efficiently. Strip malls sprang up around these bigger facilities, as did homes, businesses, and the infrastructures needed to service them—schools, hospitals, police and fire stations, restaurants, theaters, churches, and, of course, more shopping centers.

As bigger became better, a new retailing concept emerged. General merchandise stores morphed into megastores, selling virtually anything and everything. These outlets were located even farther away from city lines, literally buying the local farms and betting that consumers would come traipsing out for "everyday low prices" at stores like Wal-Mart, Kmart, Target, Sam's Club, and Price Club.

These new methods of retailing are indeed more efficient than the older ways of doing business. Nevertheless, while discount retailers are able to buy land cheap and pass the savings on to the public, we all bear the hidden environmental costs of habitat and wildlife destruction, not to mention the environmental costs associated with having to hop in the car, rather than take the bus, in order to do our shopping.

Easy Credit

It used to be that you had to "make money to spend money," and then you actually had to "spend" money to buy something. Not anymore. Thanks to credit cards, you can use up an item long before you have to pay for it. In the late 1950s and early 1960s, only the wealthiest and most creditworthy citizens were offered cards. Today, Americans receive an average of thirty-two credit-card offers annually, regardless of their credit history.

The typical card-carrying member of our society keeps 5.3 of these little plastic devils handy and ready for use. The average balance is about $4,900, and the outstanding balance on which interest is owed is almost $3,000. From a national perspective, total consumer debt in late 1997 stood at almost $1.3 trillion, a 15 percent increase since 1995. Credit-card debt alone stood at better than $520 billion, a whopping 34 percent increase during this brief two-year period.

Why do we need more credit? So we can buy more stuff! While it is debatable whether this increased consumption is really a boon to the economy (increased debt on one hand versus increased sales on the other), it certainly is not a boon to the environment. More sales mean that more resources are extracted, transported, processed, transported again, and consumed, and that at each stage more pollution is created. Since even recycling uses energy and creates pollution, there is no way around this fact.

The Paperless Office

Most of us remember how computers were going to tame the paper tiger. We were supposed to begin receiving information electronically, eliminating newspapers and magazines and, therefore, about 20 percent of all municipal solid waste (MSW) bound for landfills. All data would be stored on disks and hard drives, thus making printers, copiers, and fax machines obsolete. Businesses would send out computer disks, CD-ROMs, and videos, rather than glossy, printed brochures. Even money would begin disappearing, as paper dollars were replaced by personal IDs, billing numbers (with PINs, of course), and transactions over the Internet.

It hasn't quite happened that way. Thanks to our desire for tangible output and hard copies, along with rapidly dropping equipment prices, the number of printers, fax machines, and copiers has soared. The result has been a blizzard of paper. Between 1970 and 1994, the amount of paper and paperboard thrown away nearly doubled, from about 44 million to 81 million tons. Recyclers worked mightily to stem the tide. By recycling 28 million tons of paper in 1994 versus 6 million in 1970, they more than doubled the recycling rate for paper, from 15 to 35 percent. Despite this Herculean effort, the total quantity of paper landfilled in 1994 was 14.7 million tons *more* than all the paper landfilled in 1970. A high recycling rate was offset by the fact that more total waste was thrown away! There is no clearer example of recycling's "percentage paradox" (see chapter 2).

The problem with recycling is that it just cannot keep up! Paper is the category of material we recycle most. But since it is also the category that accounts for the greatest amount of the waste we create (about 40 percent), more paper is sent to landfills than anything else—anything! For reference, more than a third of today's landfilled MSW is paper, versus 6 percent for glass and 12 percent for plastic.

The net result is the continued use of forests as paper producers rather than as atmospheric carbon dioxide eliminators. While it may be true that paper company forests are managed for sustainable paper production, and that at least one tree is planted for each one cut down, the carbon-fixing abilities of the saplings cannot replace the capabilities lost when the bigger trees, with their larger trunks, leaf areas, and root systems, are cut down. And we can't forget to add that simply letting trees grow eliminates all the CO_2 generated in logging and related transport, production, consumption, recycling, and disposal processes.

Changing Work Patterns

Not too long ago, men went to work, and the vast majority of wives stayed home with the children. In 1960, only 19 percent of married women with children under the age of 6 worked outside the home. The Bureau of Labor Statistics estimates the current number to be 63 percent. Also, there used to be a fairly clear distinction between the suburb and the city, with people living in the former and working in the latter. But today, more than 39 million Americans work within the suburbs.

These two shifts in working patterns created major shifts in commuting that dramatically decreased the use of ride-sharing activities and helped increase the number of cars on the road. For one thing, working women still end up tending to family needs, so many must run too many errands to carpool effectively. For another, people who no longer commute into downtown usually cannot find carpool partners, as home-work arrangements are spread out among the suburbs, rather than concentrated in a city. In less than three decades the amount of carpooling has dropped dramatically, from nearly 25 percent in the 1970s to only about 8 percent today. The result is more driving, more cars, and more fuel consumption, producing more pollution and greenhouse gas emissions.

The huge increase in the number of women working away from home has also helped drive the need for convenience and fast foods. Since at-home convenience foods require more packaging and tend to be sold on a per-person basis, more waste is created. Restaurant and take-out fast food also create much more waste than the same meal at home: A family of four eating hamburgers at the kitchen table produces no postmeal packaging waste. At the restaurant, though, each person must dispose of a cup, single-serve condiment containers, and the box or wrap in which the burger was served. Further, families can eat leftovers at future meals, while restaurants must throw away food left behind.

To get a better handle on just how much more we eat away from home, consider a few numbers from the Census Bureau. Its data shows that in the very short four-year period between 1990 and 1993, the total number of eating establishments soared from 290,000 to 360,000, an increase of 25 percent. During this time, the total U.S. population grew by only about 3 percent. Yikes!

The Breakdown of the Traditional Family (or Dan Quayle Was Right)

It is fairly common knowledge that Americans are among the biggest waste generators on the planet. At 4.3 pounds of trash generated per person per day, only Canadians have the dubious honor of producing more.

While we are constantly being told exactly how much we are throwing away, very few people know why. Generally, it is left to commentators and environmentalists to point the finger at our ever-increasing, overconsumptive ways—our hollow lives, need for self-esteem, neighborly competitiveness, and so on. The truth appears to be far more mundane, and a lot more surprising.

The traditional argument goes like this: In the twenty-five years between 1970 and 1995, the amount of municipal solid waste (MSW) that was generated increased almost 70 percent, from 123 million to 208 million tons. (See table 3.1.) At the same time, our expenditures on nondurable items—the majority of everyday garbage, including disposable products and related packaging—also grew at about this rate (66 percent). Since the population grew by far less (a little over 29 percent), we must be consuming more and more stuff.

TABLE 3.1
THE MATHEMATICS OF GARBAGE

	1970	1995	PERCENT CHANGE
Population (millions)	203.3	262.8	+29.3
MSW generated (million tons)	122.6	208.0	+69.7
Nondurable goods expenditures°			
Total (billions $)	859.1	1422.5	+65.6
Per household ($)	13,550	14,369	+6.0
Households (millions)	63.4	99.0	+56.2
MSW/household (lbs.)	3867.5	4202.0	+8.6
People/household	3.2	2.7	-17.2
Durable goods expenditures°			
Total (billions $)	187.0	580.8	+210.6
Per household ($)	2950	5867	+98.9

°In 1992 dollars
Source: Statistical Abstract of the United States 1996.

From a sociological perspective, the reality is different, and becomes apparent when we look at the growth of households, rather than the growth of population. During the years cited, the number of households grew by 56 percent, almost double the rate of the population, and at a rate much more in line with solid-waste generation. Per household solid-waste increases over this quarter-century period were only about 9 percent, as were changes in per-household expenditures for nondurable goods, which rose by only 6 percent. Thus, it is household growth, much more than personal profligacy, that is driving both consumption and solid-waste generation increases.

The first question one might now ask is this: *Why has the number of households grown so dramatically?* The answer is that a wide variety of sociological factors have seriously eroded the dominance of the traditional American family, creating many family units where once there were few:

- We are much more tolerant of divorce, allowing one family to split into two or more households without the social disapproval that used to limit such activity.
- The social stigma of single parenthood has also been lifted, allowing for smaller family units, since both parents do not live under the same roof.
- People are living longer, creating an increase in smaller family units containing survivors. Further exacerbating this trend is the fact that the elderly are living by themselves or in separate units in retirement and assisted-living communities. They are not moving back in with their grown children, a common practice prior to the second half of the century.
- Our welfare system virtually forces the creation of many "splinter families." To receive maximum funding, parents must live apart and/or not with other family

members who can contribute to their well-being. This situation creates the opportunity for many unneeded, and counterproductive, housing units to form.

Because the new households are basically being formed from old ones, this situation should theoretically lead not to just more families, but smaller ones. This is exactly what has happened. The size of the average household has fallen substantially, from 3.2 people in 1970 to 2.7 in 1995 (see table 3.1). This trend has not just affected the social fabric of our society. Since smaller households are less efficient than larger ones in terms of resource use, smaller household units mean more garbage overall. As a result, a further waste-generating mechanism has been created by changes in our most basic living arrangements.

The second question to ask is this: *Why do new households create additional waste?* The answer has to do with what economists call *fixed costs*. These are the basic expenses associated with the creation of all new households. For example, think about what happens when a couple divorces. Where once there was one family with one house, one suite of furniture, one set of appliances, and one pantry, now there are two. Instead of preparing one meal with one set of dishes and utensils and one meal's worth of food and packaging, now there are two sets of everything. Ditto for cleaning supplies, lawn and garden equipment, stereos, computers, televisions, food waste, and grass clippings. Thus, the golden rule of garbage production is that *people don't create garbage, households do*.

The proof of our contention that garbage increases

mainly through new household formation, and its pressure to increase fixed costs, can be found in the area of personal expenditures for durable goods. Since cars, televisions, washing machines, and bedroom sets are among the necessities purchased by newly formed households, overall durable goods spending should rise much faster than either solid-waste, population, or household growth. As expected, the numbers do tell this tale (see table 3.1): Expenditures on durable goods during this quarter-decade were up more than 200 percent in total, and almost doubled on a per household basis!

If all of this isn't enough, houses literally create waste all by themselves. Besides a basic litany of consumer goods and durables, each household needs a physical residence. All those new homes, town houses, condos, apartments, and manufactured homes ("trailers") provide a large share of construction and demolition debris, which represents more than 30 percent of the materials lying in our landfills.

As you can see, many of our toughest environmental problems are being caused indirectly by social, cultural, and economic factors that, at first glance, are seemingly unrelated. It should also be apparent that many of the problems have arisen simply because we are consuming too many resources, not necessarily because we are throwing too much stuff away. Again, this conclusion supports the contention that we must move beyond recycling if we are to change our consumption patterns significantly in order to conserve resources.

It should also be apparent that we are not consciously or

unconsciously trying to create problems, but that we just have not taken the time to look at how the lives we lead can be positive for us and yet not so positive for our environment. This conclusion comes as a major relief, because it means that being destructive is a by-product of our activities and not part of our conscious efforts. We're not bad, we're just uninformed!

Now that we know why we think and act the way we do and what the results can be, it is time to explore how we can go about using this knowledge to our benefit. In the next chapter we take a rather novel approach to problem solving by exploring how to save Mother Nature by having human nature work for it, rather than against it.

WHAT DO WE
DO NOW?

An ounce of prevention is worth a pound of cure.
—Benjamin Franklin

If we are to conserve resources and protect the environment, it should be obvious by now that we have to change both our attitudes and our behaviors. But how? Many environmentalists and politicians believe that more legislation and regulation are the answer. We disagree: we think such steps would produce mixed results at best, and could actually backfire. For example, while Superfund legislation was designed to ensure cleanup of toxic-waste dumps, it has done little more than create slow-moving, very expensive litigation. Most of the benefit has accrued to attorneys, not to citizens or the environment.

Frankly, we Americans don't take very well to being told what we can and can't do. This is especially true when it comes to controversial and complex issues that have not yet come to a boil or created an immediate crisis that must be rallied around. We tend to react far more favorably and vigorously when we feel we have the freedom to act voluntarily and that our neighbors will behave similarly, in the best interests of all.

But getting people to act voluntarily has its pitfalls, as well. This is especially true when very bleak and frightening pictures are painted, and we are asked to change our behaviors in order to avoid the potential consequences of a doomsday scenario. This type of fear-based approach often falls flat; instead of motivating us, we feel helpless in the face of such huge problems. We then feel either powerless to act or that our efforts will prove to be futile. The result is no action at all.

The typical reaction to the issue of global warming falls in this last category. It is widely agreed that reduction of fossil-fuel usage is critical to minimizing carbon dioxide production. It is also widely known that automobiles are one of the biggest contributors to the problem. Yet each of us feels that our efforts don't count for much. Thus, we continue to buy fuel-guzzling sport-utility vehicles at an increasing rate and compound the problem by driving farther and farther each year.

Another reason that we are slow to take voluntary action is that we feel as if many environmentally related warnings have proven to be little more than fire drills and that we tend to push the panic button long before doing so is truly necessary. For example, when concern for landfill space was in full swing, politicians clamored for bans on many types of products, including disposable diapers and plastic bottles. The perception was that these items accounted for a huge percentage of what was being sent to landfills. The reality ultimately proved to be vastly different, as Garbage Project digs discovered that these two items actually account for far less than 3 percent of total landfill volume.

Another similar scenario involves chemicals in the environment. Much publicity was generated in the mid-1990s concerning the possibility that certain organic molecules were mimicking the effects of estrogen and might be the reason for the increased incidence of breast cancer in the United States. The call immediately went out for bans, litigation, and regulation. Recent studies, however, indicate that there does not appear to be a statistically positive relationship between the target chemicals and breast cancer. In fact, women whose bodies have absorbed these chemicals actually have a reduced incidence of breast cancer versus women who tested negatively for the presence of these same substances!

The effect of constant scares is that they produce quickly diminishing returns. After a while, the public starts to feel that environmentalists are crying "Wolf!" too often, with the result that all threats are discounted. This is very unfortunate because it reduces both the public's interest in matters related to environmental health and the public's resolve to help reduce the chances that disasters might occur.

This problem is very real. For example, after apple growers lost a fortune due to public overreaction concerning use of a spoilage retardant called Alar, many states enacted legislation that made disparagement of food products such as beef and produce a punishable offense. (Remember the lawsuit brought by a group of Texas cattlemen against Oprah Winfrey? The group felt she used her television show unfairly to discourage people from buying and eating meat. Fortunately, the judge didn't agree.) Thus, our ability to question, discuss, and express concern over growth and production practices in the food industry has been jeopardized, leading to the possibility that people will move on to other issues rather than risk going broke by fighting lawsuits.

The value of a fear-based approach is further reduced by the fact that people generally don't believe they are the ones who will be negatively affected by a particular problem. For example, young people have yet to come face to face with their own mortality, leading them to take risks that older people with more experience have learned to avoid. (Just watch where and when a group of college students will cross the street, or how they drive.) On the other hand, there is a tendency for older people to become set in their ways, which also reduces the odds that they will react rationally to risk. (Next time there is a major flood that destroys some Mississippi River town, watch the news footage of interviews with victims. Most of those who remained in their homes are the elderly, who had seen it all before and steadfastly refused to leave the place where they had lived for years, believing that yet again disaster would not happen to them.)

Finally, we must account for the fact that people don't easily make voluntary sacrifices if they don't think there is a significant personal reward in doing so. This is especially problematic in our society because our standard of living is so high. When we compare what we think we have to gain by sacrifice versus what we have to lose, we generally conclude that the best personal course of action is to maintain the status quo.

This is a natural and very rational way to think. History has shown that revolutions occur because those who have nothing to lose are willing to fight for change, while those who have nothing to gain fight to keep things as they are. The Cuban, Russian, and French revolutions all illustrate this point, as it was the proletariat who rose up to defeat the ruling classes and turn the "haves" into the "have nots," and vice versa.

If none of our more typical approaches work, what should we do?

Go with the Flow

Virtually everything in nature follows the path of least resistance. For example, water seeks its own level and flows downhill. Electricity "seeks" to return to a grounded state, as do the electrons circulating around the nucleus of atoms.

Human beings generally take the path of least resistance, too. This is obvious when you look at the typical American diet, filled with what's easiest and most pleasant for us to eat, rather than what is really best for us. The same can be said for sitting on the couch versus exercising or saving money for tomorrow versus spending it today.

"Going with the flow" is also evident when it comes to social issues. The reason welfare reform now seems to be working is that we have finally made it easier for people to work than to receive benefits by not doing so. Thus, all things being equal, people do what's easiest. It is up to society to recognize this fact and design systems and programs that make the expected course of action the most rewarding among the various alternatives, both legal and illegal.

Based upon the way in which humans are both programmed and willing to act, we believe that positive change occurs when programs adhere to the following six guidelines:

1. *Be positive and upbeat.* It is extremely important to provide solutions and not just problems. A doom-and-gloom approach just serves to discourage and decrease motivation.
2. *Make the issue personally relevant.* Our mental processes cause us to evaluate virtually all decisions by asking, "What's in it for me?" Make sure people understand the personal payoff they will gain by participating.
3. *Keep things simple.* We don't handle complexity very well. If programs must be long and complicated, break them down into easy-to-understand chunks, steps, or stages.
4. *Set and communicate a specific goal.* We work better when we have a target to shoot at. Give people a specific objective over a specific period of time. Paint a pic-

ture of the outcome so that people can "see" it in their minds and internalize it.

5. *Make the project fun.* Oh, how we love to be entertained!

6. *Provide ongoing feedback and rewards.* It is important for people to feel that progress is being made and that they be applauded for their efforts. (Don't overdo it, though, since too much reinforcement can actually reduce motivation!)

Change Behavior, Not Attitudes (or Actions Speak Louder Than Words)

When groups embark on public information campaigns, their goal is usually to change people's attitudes, assuming that once opinions change, so, too, will behaviors. But savvy marketers have learned that while counterintuitive, the opposite is true! Sometimes it is easier first to change people's behaviors and hope that attitudes will follow suit.

There are two concepts in social psychology that confirm what these marketers have learned. Both *self-perception theory* and *cognitive dissonance theory* predict that many times the best way to change an opinion is first to change a behavior. In a classic study at Yale University, a group of liberal students was asked to write an essay supporting a conservative candidate running for president. Students were given various amounts of money for doing so, and their attitudes regarding the candidate were measured before and after writing the essays. It turned out that once the essays had been written, opinions toward the candidate become more favorable in inverse proportion to the amount of money offered. Thus, those who were paid the least changed the most, and vice versa. The reason was that students who attributed their writing the essay to the fact that they received significant money didn't change their attitudes very much. But those who received little money attributed their being able to write such a positive essay to the fact that, deep down, they must really like the candidate, since they had no significant external incentive to do so.

We all see this theory at work every day. Manufacturers provide us with free trial sizes of new products because they know that if we try the product and like it, the odds that we will purchase it go way up. After all, we didn't ask to receive the free item, so we were under no obligation to use it. Once we did try it, we convinced ourselves that we really wanted to use it, and thus our decision to buy followed suit.

Practice Source Reduction, or Using Less Stuff

As Benjamin Franklin once wrote, "An ounce of prevention is worth a pound of cure." When applied to resource conservation, prevention is technically known as source reduction and occurs *before* something bad happens. A pound of cure describes recycling, which occurs *after* an event, in this case consumption, has occurred.

To put it in today's terms, imagine that you and a friend go to a bar together. You have two beers, your friend has eight. The next morning, you feel just fine, while your friend has to take a few aspirin to cure a hangover. Obviously, your choice was the better one, since it's better to prevent problems than to have to figure out how to fix them. Using less stuff is like prevention. Overconsumption followed by aspirin is like recycling. Which strategy makes more sense? Costs less? Is less painful?

When looking at this example, it is important to remember that the hangover remedy didn't really solve the problem of heavy drinking, but merely mitigated its short-term effects. Long term, your friend still runs the risk of severe medical problems, such as cirrhosis of the liver. Along these same lines, when you realize that consumption is the primary factor affecting the environment, you can more easily grasp the fact that recycling really *is* just like taking aspirin. It may make us feel a bit better today, but it still doesn't get to the root of the truly important ecological problems facing tomorrow: habitat destruction, loss of biodiversity, greenhouse gas production, and environmental degradation. In fact, by allowing us to take our eyes off these problems, recycling might actually hinder our efforts to solve them!

A big part of the reason that using less stuff is so powerful is that, unlike recycling, its effects are felt during the entire "cradle to grave" lifespan of a product—from the beginning to the end of the production/consumption/ disposal chain. When you use less to start with, not only are fewer materials needed but less energy is used to create and transport those materials. And with less production and transportation come less pollution and greenhouse gas generation as well. Using less is thus vastly more powerful than recycling, since the latter is employed primarily at the end of the cycle, long after initial production as well as after product transportation, storage, and use.

When applied scientifically, this type of thinking can help us better understand the true sources and impacts of waste. Known as Life Cycle Analysis, this raw-material extraction to final disposal methodology can really open our eyes as to where the real waste occurs, and thus where the most effort in reducing it should be placed. Consider one of America's favorite foods, the hamburger:

Let's say that you've just finished having lunch at your favorite fast-food place. You get up from the table and take the tray to the trash receptacle. As you open the little swinging door and watch the garbage glide into the waiting bin, you notice how high the wrappers, bags, boxes, and cups have piled. "What a waste," you think. "Why can't this place recycle some of this packaging?"

But in reality, how much of the waste and resources used for your lunch are represented by what you see in the trash? 60 percent? 70 percent? 80? How about 1 percent! Approximately 99 percent of all the waste actually occurs before you even eat the burger! "How," you might ask, "is that possible?"

We'll begin with the bun, which is principally flour. Flour starts out as grain, which has to be grown using water, fertilizer, pesticides, herbicides, and sometimes fungicides. These chemicals enhance agricultural efficiency, but they also create water-pollution problems if and when rains cause them to "run off" into nearby streams, lakes, and aquifers. The production of these chemicals may cause pollution and use up lots of energy as well.

The grain is planted as seed, grown and harvested using tractors, threshers, reapers, and combines. It took plenty of raw materials (and created plenty of waste) to manufacture these machines, and it takes plenty of fuel to keep them running. And while running, they produce air pollutants and greenhouse gases.

The grain is transported by truck or rail to storage sites, milled into flour, stored again, and then sent to bakeries. Milling and baking require energy to produce dough and buns, which are then wrapped and shipped to fast-food stores. Between every step, the transportation process burns fuel and again produces pollutants.

Other farm products that went into your burger include tomatoes, onions, cucumbers, and lettuce. The tomatoes and cucumbers required further processing to be turned into ketchup and pickles, respectively.

You might ask, "Where's the beef?" Once again, we start with grain, which is used for feed. After vast amounts of food and water are fed to cattle, it's off to the stockyard for sale and then on to the processing plant. At the plant, cattle are slaughtered and rendered, with the beef being cut, packaged, cooled, and shipped to warehouses in refrigerator cars and trucks. Every step in the process, especially refrigeration, is energy intensive. And don't forget all the animal wastes from feedlots that often go directly back into the environment, in bulk.

At the warehouse, the meat is aged, ground into patties, boxed, frozen, and stored. It is then shipped in freezer trucks to restaurants where it's kept cold until ready to cook (with energy, of course). At this point, the bun, patty, condiments, and packaging all come together to bring you the final product.

We should also point out the resources needed to produce the wrappers and boxes themselves. Paper is processed from trees, using large amounts of water, chemicals, and nonrenewable resources. Plastic is processed from oil or natural gas, also utilizing nonrenewable resources. Both materials require energy to produce and ship, resulting in more carbon dioxide generation and air or water pollution. And of course, these materials are created using processes that produce solid waste as well.

By now, it should be very apparent that the resources used and waste generated at stages we don't see are far greater than those we do notice when confronting the restaurant's trash bin. There are the pollutants and greenhouse gases created when energy is used for planting, harvesting, transporting, milling, baking, rendering, cleaning, refrigerating, freezing, and cooking. There is also all the packaging used when shipping and purchasing seed, fertilizer, pesticides, fungicides, beef, buns, and condiments.

❖   ❖   ❖

Obviously, the results of our mini Life Cycle Analysis are an eye-opener for most people. Doing this type of work shows us that the true way to reduce waste is to eat the special sauce, lettuce, cheese, pickles, onions on the sesame seed bun and skip the beef. (Sorry, McDonald's, but we couldn't resist.) The reason is that each link in the food chain—from plants to animals to humans—increases resource use by a factor of 10. In other words, it takes 10 pounds of grain to produce 1 pound of meat! This means that a more vegetarian lifestyle could save up to 90 percent of food resources and reduce an equal amount of waste. So the next time you head for a fast-food place and are feeling concern for the environment, skip the burger and belly up to the salad bar.

Another one of the benefits of using less stuff is that it saves lots of money, since what doesn't get produced doesn't get paid for. Also, there are no disposal or environmental cleanup costs to deal with if nothing is created. On the other hand, continuing our current usage of resources and then recycling can cost a great deal of money. The citizens of Ann Arbor, Michigan, for example, were rather surprised to discover that it is far more expensive to recycle trash than to throw it away. A recent bidding war for the town's recycling program brought to light the fact that it costs about $1.8 million to maintain the program, yet the materials collected for recycling produced only about $100,000 in revenues to offset that cost. The town decided to recycle anyway, because it felt it was the right thing to do. That's fine with us. If towns feel there is a moral value to recycling and they can afford to do so, more power to them. But the next time someone tells you that "there's gold in them thar garbage hills," you might want to remind him or her that while gold is going for $300 an ounce, recyclables, on average, are selling for a penny a pound.

The final reason to use less stuff is that doing so actually improves the rate at which we recycle and, more important, reduces the amount of trash both generated and ultimately discarded in landfills. This last point is critical because from a conservation viewpoint, *the best way to reduce any environmental impact is not to recycle more, but to produce and dispose of less.*

A look at table 4.1 will clarify this point. Using round numbers to describe today's recycling rate of about 27 percent, we recycle 55 million out of the approximately 205 million tons of trash we generate. This means that about 150 million tons of waste are sent to landfills or incinerators. With the market for most recyclable materials fairly mature, there is not much chance of getting the rate up by recycling significantly more paper, plastic, glass, or metal. Further, there is currently a glut of available materials, with pricing down 50 percent in the past two years. With more and more towns and cities looking to recycle, this supply/demand scenario is not likely to change anytime soon.

Given the current situation, it is expected that growth in the volume of recyclable materials will be moderate at best, say, an additional 5 million tons a year over the next few years. With total trash generation also growing to about 215 million tons, the recycling rate will increase only

1 percent, meaning that the most important figure—the stuff we can't reuse or recycle and therefore must bury—will increase to about 155 million tons.

But look at what happens if we work to reduce total trash generated by 10 percent. Volume would fall to 185 million tons. Let's say that much of this decrease was due to a reduction in recyclable packaging, so that recyclable volume remained flat at 55 million tons. The new recycling rate would actually jump to 30 percent, while the net amount of trash that would have to be landfilled would fall to 130 million tons. This is the exact opposite of the "Recycling Percentage Paradox." In this scenario, the recycling rate is not only higher, but the amount of stuff landfilled is lower!

TABLE 4.1
THE VALUE OF CREATING LESS WASTE
IN THE FIRST PLACE

WASTE STATISTICS FOR THE UNITED STATES

	Generated (million tons)	Recycled (million tons)	Landfilled (million tons)	Recycling rate (%)
Current in 1998	205	55	150	27
Expected by 2000	215	60	155	28
Using 10% less by 2000	185	55	130	30

Note: For purposes of simplification and comprehension, numbers have been rounded.

Thus, while recycling is good, using less in the first place is better. Using less not only helps increase the rate of recycling but, most importantly, significantly helps conserve resources by decreasing the amount of stuff that is ultimately thrown away.

Here's How We Can Do It

Getting people to recycle is fairly simple. People aren't asked to change what or how they buy things, merely to change how they throw things away. Thus, it's easy to feel good about putting empty containers into blue or green bins, taking the bins to the curb, and watching the stuff being picked up and diverted from the landfill.

But how do you get people excited about buying and using less stuff, which is the absence of a negative, at best, and seems so un-American, at worst? The answer is to hit people where it counts—in their wallets and their hearts. The secret to getting lots of people to use less is to remind them that not buying what they don't need, and shopping more efficiently, saves the modern world's two scarcest resources: time and money.

Do saving time and money pass the acid test by fitting in with the six points previously mentioned? We certainly think so:

- The message itself is a positive one, and highly relevant to virtually all of us.
- The concept is simple and easy to understand.
- Goals can be established regarding how much time and money can be saved, and over what period.

- Saving is fun, since it means we have more resources available to do things we might otherwise not get to do.
- Finally, there is definitely a built-in feedback mechanism to saving: you can measure progress along the way and realize that the more you save, the better quality of life you can build for yourself and your family.

When it comes to providing incentives to reduce, many communities are putting theory to work by charging residents for the amount of garbage they wish to throw away. Generally known as Pay-As-You-Throw, or PAYT for short, these programs charge households for trash collection by the bag—the more you throw away, the more you pay.

Results have generally been favorable, especially for mid-size communities: the amount of trash left for pickup has generally declined significantly, as citizens find ways to reduce waste and the cost of collection. Interestingly, PAYT programs help increase recycling collection as well, since there's a direct economic savings to be had by putting those cans, bottles, and papers in the recycling bin rather than the trash can. (You can find out more about PAYT by calling the EPA's toll-free Helpline at 888-EPA-PAYT.)

Now that we know why we must use less stuff, it's time to find out how.

USE LESS STUFF WHEN SHOPPING

When the going gets tough, the tough go shopping.
—Anonymous

Most of the stuff we buy comes from the market, so this seems like a good place to start our journey. But before we can, there's a little something we have to do at home first: make a list. It may sound trite, but *shopping from a list may be your best weapon in the war on waste, since it ensures that you buy what you need and nothing more.* Go through the fridge, freezer, and cupboards to see what you need for the week's meals and write the items down. Do the same in the cleaning closet and laundry room. (Use the back of an envelope or some other piece of wastepaper.)

Now that you have a list, it's time for step number 2: *stick to it.* Don't be tempted by specials, sales, and promotions that don't relate to what's on the list. Buying things that don't get used or eaten, and ultimately get thrown away, is a major source of food and other household waste.

One more thing before you leave the house: consider taking along cash, rather than checks or credit cards, to make your purchases. You can really feel it when you spend cold, hard cash. It may hurt more to count the bills out to the cashier, but it will save money in the long run. In addition, by having only a given limit of available funds, you will reduce the risk of overspending. Checks are the next best alternative, and credit cards the last option, since it's so easy to buy today and not see the bill until tomorrow or next month.

At the Store

Your first major decision doesn't relate to what you buy, but is just as important: do you need a big cart, or will one of those small baskets with a handle suffice? Don't laugh! Experience shows that Parkinson's Law of Garbage applies here as well as it does for the trash containers of Beverly Hills: the more room available for purchases, the more purchases will be made. (That's why you may have noticed that produce bags are getting bigger. Stores learned through research that people buy more fruits and vegetables when given bigger bags in which to put the stuff.) If nature abhors a vacuum, humans abhor an empty bag, box, or cart.

OK, you've got quite a lot of stuff to buy, so you opt for the cart. Now it's time to run the gauntlet of store specials, put right up front to entice you to get in the swing of purchasing cereal, soda, or cookies. These are all very profitable items for retailers. If you see something you were going to buy anyway, fine. Otherwise, just say no. Remember: *stick to the list.* And if you do buy, don't purchase more than you can use before it spoils. Otherwise, you've created a false economy *and* wasted resources.

First Stop, the Produce Aisle

It's the first section in most stores for two big reasons. First, all of that fresh food looks healthy and gets us in the mood to purchase. Second, fruits and vegetables aren't generally the key to getting people into a store, so it makes sense to put them up front. (Designwise, stores put their "must have" items in the back, so that you're forced to travel the whole store to find them, with the hope that you'll stop and pick up other things along the way. This is why milk, an item that people are forever stopping to pick up, is almost always at the back corner of the store.)

Follow these tips and you'll purchase what you need with a minimum amount of waste and money:

> Buy fruit based on when you expect to use it. If you are buying bananas but aren't planning to eat them for a few days, pick a bunch that's still a little green.
> Do the math and you'll buy less. If you only need one lemon but the sign says 4 for 99 cents (or 25 cents

each for singles), you will only save a penny if you buy all four. There's no great savings in doing so; in fact, you'll lose 75 cents if you end up throwing three away.

Steer clear of produce specials, unless you're prepared to eat the stuff when you get home. Sale items are usually on the verge of being too ripe to sell, so the store is trying to entice you to buy so they don't have to throw away the stuff and take a loss. (Notice to banana bread and applesauce makers: disregard this advice. Since recipes call for overripe ingredients, now is the time to buy!)

Skip the extra packaging. Casabas, cantaloupes, cucumbers, and corn come in their own natural packages and don't need paper or plastic trays, thank you.

Pack Fruit and Vegetables in as Few Bags as Possible

If charged by weight for produce, put items that cost the same per pound in one bag. Also, items that are charged for by the unit (e.g., 3 for $1.00) can be put in the same sack as well—the checkout person will have no problem telling the difference between three apples and six oranges.

Speaking of bags, those packaged salads jamming produce shelves today are actually a good thing, environmentally speaking. First, there is no food waste, since everything in the bag is edible, and the yucky parts get chopped up for animal feed. Second, the weight of the packaging is more than offset by the weight of the peels, off-color leaves, and stems that your family wouldn't have eaten and would thus have been tossed out. There is even evidence that these salads may be healthier than made-from-scratch versions; they've been fully washed and then packaged in such a way that the vegetables retain their nutrients longer than if the ingredients were simply hauled to market and put on the shelves.

Dry Goods, Household Cleaners, Pet Foods

There are many things that you can do throughout the store that will save money and natural resources. Since about 500 pounds of packaging is discarded annually per person in America, we are especially concerned with reducing its impact at the landfill. If each of us reduced our packaging consumption by 10 percent, we would reduce the total amount of trash created in the United States by 6.3 million tons, or 12.5 billion pounds, per year. This is equivalent to a little over one and a half weeks' worth of the garbage generated nationally in this country.

We've grouped the key ideas into five main strategies:

1. *Concentrate!* Concentrated products help the environment by reducing their weight and thus the amount of energy it takes to transport them. Less energy used means less pollution and lower greenhouse gas emissions. The result is that, in most cases, you also save money because you add the water at home and receive some of the benefit from reduced transportation costs. You also receive the advantage of your groceries weighing less, making them easier to carry.

Concentrates really make packaging very efficient. Let's look at juice as an example. If you buy juice in a glass bottle, by weight you get about 65 percent juice and 35 percent glass. Since a little less than one-quarter of all glass is recycled, it is fair to say that about 26 percent of the combined weight of the juice and container heads to the landfill.

If you've bought juice in bottles, save them. Next time you go to the store, purchase juice concentrate in either aseptic packages (juice boxes) or aluminum cans. At home, reuse your glass bottle by dumping in the concentrate and adding water. When you take this approach, you end up with 99 percent juice and only 1 percent package to be thrown away or recycled. That's because (*a*) the concentrate package weighs virtually nothing compared to the finished product, and (*b*) you kept the glass container out of the garbage, to be reused over and over. This little system of using concentrates to reuse and reduce decreases the trash created by a factor of 25 times. To the average family using a bottle of juice a week, we're talking about a savings of 50 pounds of garbage and $25 per year. Not bad for one little item! (If you haven't already been doing this, you can now offset the cost of this book and then some.)

Many other products are available in concentrated form: powdered and liquid laundry detergent, fabric softener, dishwashing liquid, and various cleaners all come to mind. Don't let the small size of the containers fool you, either. These products are just as potent as the bigger non-concentrated versions to which you don't add water. Keep this fact in mind, especially with laundry detergents. Many people use more than the directions call for because they're afraid that the concentratated versions aren't as good as the old-fashioned ones. Not true. By not following the directions, you're wasting money and resources. You're also making more money for the manufacturer and the retailer, since you end up buying more product than you need.

2. *Buy refills.* Refill packages reduce waste for three reasons most of us don't normally consider. First, they are usually larger than the original packages and thus contain more product per ounce of package. Second, they contain less material, since (*a*) they are often made of thinner material than the original container, and (*b*) don't include spouts, pumps or spray tops. Third, these containers usually contain a layer of recycled materials, saving on the use of new or "virgin" materials.

Refillable products include liquid soap, window cleaners, hand lotion, carpet cleaners, and laundry detergents. Better yet, many of the refill products are concentrated, further reducing waste and saving you money.

3. *Be flexible!* Flexible packaging is just like regular packaging, but much thinner, lighter, and less bulky. Thus, the packaging itself uses less stuff and saves on transportation energy as well. From an engineering standpoint, flexible packages—bags, pouches, aseptic boxes, and foil "brick packs"—are environmental superstars, providing you with much more product per unit of packaging.

Examples of these types of containers include foil bricks used for coffee and nuts; pouches that contain snack foods or cleaner refills; aseptic boxes for juice, soy milk, and tomato sauce; and bags of cereal that replace the traditional bag-in-box variety. Purchasing the latter can really save resources: a year's worth of cereal purchased in bags versus boxes will reduce waste by 15 pounds and your food bill by $50.

4. *Buy in bulk.* The laws of physics stipulate that as containers get larger, the volume of what's in them increases faster than the volume of the containers themselves. In plain English, this means that as packages get bigger, you get proportionately more product and less waste. Thus, it makes environmental sense and saves economic cents to buy in bulk.

If you normally buy two half-gallon milk containers, switch to the gallon size. The same goes for items like flour, sugar, rice, pasta, ketchup, and pet food. One word of caution, though: don't buy more of something than you can use up before it goes bad.

5. *Buy dry.* This is a similar concept to buying concentrates. Because you add your own water, you save transportation energy and reduce the amount of packaging per serving. This is especially good advice in the pet food aisle, where you can buy huge bags of dry food versus itty-bitty cans of moist food. And dry can even be better for your pet's health—ask your vet. The same thinking applies to soup mixes, powdered soft drinks, and pancake mixes.

Meat, Dairy, and Deli

You're in the homestretch. The key to using less stuff in these rather high-waste departments is to reduce the chance of spoilage. There are many simple, yet effective, ways to do so:

First, check freshness dates. Buy items with the farthest-away "use by" dates, ensuring that the food is in good condition now and will remain edible until cooked.

Don't buy exotic cuts of meat or unusual types of fish, unless you're sure your family will eat them. Garbage Project research shows that we waste a larger percentage of unfamiliar items than we do of foods with which we are well acquainted.

Deli items tend to spoil quickly, so it's better to purchase a little less than a little more. When buying cold cuts, tell the person behind the counter that you only want a certain weight and no more. This should help reduce the inclination to give you more than you asked for, and for you to accept the additional amount.

If you're buying fresh meat or seafood, check the date it was packed or the last possible date of sale, either of which is printed on the wrapper. Then, trust your senses. Fish that smells funny is probably old. Ditto for beef and poultry.

Need cheese? Skip the individually wrapped slices. Unless your family regularly takes individual slices to school or work for lunch, what's the point of the extra packaging?

Checking Out

Now it's time for that nail-biter question: paper or plastic? It turns out that it's basically your choice, since both have environmental advantages and disadvantages. Paper bags are made from renewable resources, but use a lot of them. Plastic bags are made from nonrenewable sources, but use fewer total resources to produce and transport. Paper bags are four times bulkier than plastic bags—and Garbage Project digs have documented that neither one will biodegrade in most landfills. Both types, however, are recyclable and reusable.

So whichever bags you take, be sure to reuse them. Paper bags are great for keeping newspapers neatly stored for recycling days, make excellent book covers and even gift wrap—have the kids decorate the paper with crayons or markers. Plastic sacks make good trash-can liners, lunch bags, and gym-clothes carriers.

Here are a few more checkout-time waste-reduction tips:

If you can bring your own bags from home, do so. Environmentally, of course, the best answer is to take your own cloth or net bags, but reusing paper or plastic bags is an excellent option. Since storing and remembering to bring a number of bags from home can be difficult, scrunch up a few plastic bags you've just unloaded and put them in your car's glove compartment *now*.

Take as few bags as you can comfortably handle. Speaking of handles, bulky liquids like milk, orange juice, and bleach have their own. Skip the bag.

Pack wisely to prevent food damage. Store baggers will usually put the heavy stuff, like canned goods, on the bottom. They almost always make sure bread and eggs go on top, so they're not crushed or broken. Be on the lookout, just in case!

Pack refrigerated and frozen foods together, so they stay cold.

Bag meats and cleaners separately, in plastic. In the first case, you'll keep juices from ruining other items. In the second instance, you'll keep potentially noxious chemicals away from your foodstuffs.

Try not to double-bag. Today's sacks, both paper and plastic, are usually strong enough to do the job one at a time.

Back Home

There are still a few simple things to do when you get home and unpack your groceries:

If you bought large quantities of meats, break them down into smaller, meal-sized units and store appropriately. For example, if you have a family of four and just purchased two pounds of hamburger meat, you might want to separate it into two one-pound packages. That way, you won't waste half when you end up making only four hamburgers. Store the other half in the freezer and label with the date purchased and type of meat.

Rotate foods in your pantry, refrigerator, and freezer. Check the dates and make sure those with the shortest time to expiration are in the front and within easy reach, and that those items that will last longer are more toward the back.

Store the grocery bags in a place where they are easy to reach, available to be used again.

That was all pretty easy, wasn't it? And as we promised, you saved money while reducing quite a bit of waste. Wait until you see how easy it is to save at home and how many opportunities there are to do so!

AROUND THE HOUSE

Much of the waste we're typically concerned with around
our homes relates to packaging and food. We covered
much about packaging in the last chapter, and are saving
food for the next one. But there are two important items
we waste regularly, and give little thought to, since the
excess doesn't go into the trash can: water and energy.

To many of us, water seems plentiful. Yet in many areas
of the country, especially in the Southwest and parts of

California, water is a scarce and precious resource, usually brought in from miles away. Further, there are many places in the world (including Los Angeles) where the population has outstripped the natural carrying capacity of the local environment, making water rationing a reality. It is even postulated that future wars in areas such as the Near East and parts of Eurasia may be fought not over religion, politics, or culture, but over water rights and availability.

Energy, too, seems abundant. But what we don't see is the fact that energy usually comes from turning some type of matter into electricity. In most cases, this matter comes from fossil fuels such as coal, oil, or natural gas. These are nonrenewable and will eventually be depleted. (We will replace them as best we can with other options as their dwindling supply makes them too expensive for large-scale use.) In developing nations, many people and power plants burn wood or charcoal, which are renewable resources, but particularly inefficient ones. In addition, in most such countries, wood is being burned at a much faster rate than it is being replenished.

Regardless of whether they are renewable or not, there is a large environmental price to pay for using all these fuels. Burning produces large amounts of carbon dioxide and varying amounts of carbon monoxide, nitrous and nitric oxide, and sulfur dioxide. Burning wood, coal, and charcoal can also produce particulates, which are unhealthy to breathe, especially for the elderly and those with conditions such as asthma. We also have to remember that mining coal can leave ugly scars on the land, while clearing forests for fuel—as is currently happening in many developing nations—destroys habitats and reduces biodiversity.

Besides reducing water and energy consumption at home, there is one other big way to help preserve the environment: routine maintenance. By keeping your appliances and machinery in top running condition, you'll maximize their efficiency as well as their service life. Doing so will save money on energy and replacement costs, as well as saving big old equipment and big new boxes from the trash heap.

Let's go through your house, room by room, and see what we can do in this regard.

The Kitchen

There is plenty of room to improve energy and water efficiency in most kitchens. We'll start with the appliances.

REFRIGERATOR

Try to locate or move the fridge away from heat-producing appliances, such as the stove. Also, move it out of direct sunlight, and away from heat vents.

Make sure the refrigerator is level, and that the area around the grill and any vents is both clean and clear. The key is to keep the coils on the bottom or at the back as clean as possible by removing dust and lint. Doing so will make your fridge much more efficient, meaning that it will use less energy and last longer, too—a double savings. For reference, just one-hundredth of an inch of dust or dirt on the coils can reduce efficiency by 5 percent.

Wipe moisture from containers and cover liquids. Excess humidity makes the compressor run longer.

Try raising the temperature in both the refrigerator and freezer a bit. Don't go overboard, since it's not worth saving a little energy if you're wasting a whole lot of food through spoilage.

Let hot dishes cool down prior to placing them in the fridge or freezer.

Full freezers and refrigerators run more efficiently, since the cold food inside helps keep the temperature down. If the appliances are nearly empty, fill plastic milk jugs with water and place inside. This works especially well in the freezer, but be careful not to overfill the jug, since water expands as it freezes.

Check any water lines for leaks and be especially careful not to rupture these lines when moving the unit for cleaning.

Check and clean the rubber seals around the door to make sure they close tightly.

DISHWASHER

Run the dishwasher only when full, since it always uses the same amount of water, no matter how many dishes, pots, pans, and silverware are being washed.

Look for a unit that has low water usage, in the 7- to

9-gallon range. You'll not only save water but energy, too, since 80 percent of energy consumed by a dishwasher is for water heating.

Use the right cycle. Rarely will you need to use the one for pots and pans, so stick with the light and regular cycles. Both use far less water.

Don't bother prerinsing dishes that contain only a normal amount of residue. Prerinsing just uses up additional hot water. Run through a load with a range of debris—light to heavy and caked-on. That way, you'll know the look of what you need to prerinse.

If available, use the no-heat fan or air-dry setting. To ensure that dishes dry, run the machine before going to bed so that items have all night to dry.

Check the filter at the bottom regularly, and remove any debris.

Unless your machine is ancient, it can probably be repaired rather than replaced. Call for service before you go shopping for a new unit.

OVEN, STOVE, AND COOKWARE

Cover pots with lids to prevent up to two-thirds of potential heat loss.

Use a pressure cooker if appropriate. Cooking time is reduced dramatically and energy usage is reduced by 50 to 75 percent.

Use the smallest pots and pans necessary, and make sure that the bottom is flat. You want maximum contact with the burners.

If several dishes require about the same oven temperature, cook them all in one oven at one time.

Turn the oven off a few minutes before the food is cooked and let the heat already in the oven finish it.

Check and clean oven seals to ensure a tight fit.

THE SINK

Make sure the faucet doesn't drip. Usually a washer or a few turns with a wrench will do the trick.

Check the fittings under the sink to ensure no leaks occur there, either.

If you have an instant-hot or instant-cold appliance, fiddle with the settings so that you get water that meets your needs, but no more. This will reduce energy usage.

The best way to deal with clogged drains is to prevent them. Use the screen on the drain plug regularly, and you'll reduce the need to purchase and pour expensive and potentially hazardous chemical drain openers.

Another way to keep drains clean is to pour in a clump of baking soda, then add a cup of white vinegar. Wait one minute, then flush with hot water. This is much cheaper and safer than using chemical cleaners.

Don't use running water to thaw food; it is wasteful and can ruin the texture and taste of whatever you are defrosting. Fill the sink with cold water and let the food sit in it until thawed.

The Bathroom

Water, water everywhere! And it's easy to keep so much from going down the drain!

Make sure faucets in the sink, shower, and tub don't drip.

Don't leave the water running when you brush your teeth.

When shaving with a blade, fill the sink basin with hot water instead of letting the water run.

Speaking of shaving with a blade, try using soap rather than shaving cream to lather up. If it works, you may never need to buy more of the lather again.

When done shaving, clean and dry the blades. Wet blades corrode and lose their edge faster than dry ones. Graham Kerr, TV's "Galloping Gourmet," confided in us once that he used the same "disposable razor" to shave fifty-six times to prove it could be done! You don't have to prove it again.

If the water is too steamy, turn down the hot a bit instead of turning up the cold.

Take showers rather than baths. (It is important to make an exception for people who use baths as a form of stress reduction. Reduce the number of times you use the technique to the minimum; but if it works for you, use it!) Showers use about 50 percent less water than baths. If you already take showers, try to take shorter and slightly cooler ones.

Check to make sure your showerheads contain flow restrictors, which cut down water use without significantly reducing pressure. If you need them, they can be purchased very cheaply at hardware stores. In some areas, the water company will give them to you for free.

Fill a half-gallon plastic milk jug with water and put it in the tank behind your toilet. At eight flushes a day, you'll save over 100 gallons a year.

Check the toilet for leaks by adding a few drops of food coloring to the tank. Wait five minutes and check the bowl for dye. If the water in the bowl becomes colored, have a plumber fix the leak. Even an imperceptible one can waste 40 or more gallons a day.

If installing a new toilet, use an ultra-low-flush (ULF) model that can save over 5 gallons per flush versus older models—at eight flushes per day that would save 14,600 gallons of water in one year!

Try cleaning sinks and toilets with baking soda and a brush. This will save money and reduce the use of hazardous chemicals.

Buy multiple-use products, such as shampoo and hair conditioner in one. This reduces the number of items, packages, and costs associated with hair care.

Purchase toothpaste and deodorants in stand-alone containers with no outer packaging. Most major brands have versions of their products that don't use paperboard boxes.

Family, Recreation, Work Areas

Turn off computers, TVs, VCRs, and so forth, when not in use.

Replace batteries in remote-control units with rechargeables. Ditto for toys, cameras, and the like. We throw away over 2.5 billion batteries a year, or around 10 per person. Once landfilled, batteries can corrode and leach toxic chemicals into the earth and groundwater. Rechargeables significantly reduce both waste and the need for new batteries to be manufactured and purchased. (*Caution:* As environmentally friendly as they are, don't use rechargeables in items that you must rely on, like smoke detectors. Rechargeables lose 1 percent of their power per day, whether they are used or not.)

Donate old sports and computer equipment to the PTA, Salvation Army, or some other organization. Or, sell equipment to stores that specialize in used items. Chains such as Play It Again Sports and Computer Renaissance will be happy to buy these types of equipment.

Reuse old videotapes instead of buying new ones. After all, how many times will you watch Cousin Freddie get married?

If your children have stopped playing with a toy, put it in the closet for a few months. When you take it out, it will seem new again. This should help reduce the frequency of toy purchases. Eventually, however, every toy will lose its magic or be outgrown. If you don't have younger kids about to grow into it, give the toy to a charitable outfit or try to sell it at a reuse store.

Basement/Attic

Believe it or not, these two rooms are where the real ULS (use less stuff) action is. Most of the heavy energy-using appliances reside in the basement, while a great deal of needless energy loss occurs in the attic. Here's what to do:

PIPES

Insulate all hot-water pipes coming from the water heater, as well as all pipes coming from and leading back to a steam or hot-water boiler. It's easy to do with either foam or precut fiberglass insulation. Both are cut to fit around pipes.

Check gas pipes for leaks. If you suspect a leak (the smell is obvious), call your utility company immediately. You can try and find it yourself by doing what the pros do: fill a spray bottle used for window or household cleaners with a solution of water and dishwasher soap. Spray pipe joints and watch for bubbling. If it occurs, you've got a leak. (Don't panic, but do put out any smoking material! In fact, don't have any cigarettes lit in these areas at any time.)

HEATING/COOLING

Have your furnace cleaned and adjusted regularly in order to maximize efficiency and minimize the chance of carbon monoxide emissions. Up to 80 percent of all heating and cooling compressor problems could be eliminated through preventive and timely maintenance.

If you have a boiler, "blow down" the system once a week. Ask your local service center to show you the blow-down valve on your boiler and how to use it. Doing so will get the gunk out of the system, keeping your boiler efficient and helping it to last much longer.

At the end of the season, turn off the furnace. No need to use fuel to keep the pilot light burning during the late spring through early fall.

If you have a forced-air system, change the filter at least once a year. This will make your unit much more efficient. The dollar or so spent on this today will yield many dollars in savings tomorrow.

Regularly clean out ducts. Also, make sure they are tight fitting, and insulate them.

The same applies for central air-conditioning systems. Change the filter regularly and have the unit inspected to ensure it is properly charged. By the way, Freon or similar gases should never need to be replaced. If you regularly have to add it, chances are good that there's a leak in the system that needs to be repaired. Also, if the system does have to be charged, make sure it's done properly. An undercharge of just

10 percent can increase operating costs and energy consumption by almost 20 percent.

Keeping the air-conditioning compressor in top shape is also important. Up to 80 percent of all air-conditioning compressor failures could be avoided if problems were corrected when first noticed. While you're at it, make sure the unit is clean. Dirt on coils, the blower, and other critical parts can increase electrical usage by about 50 percent.

Use ceiling and other fans for comfort in occupied rooms. They use very small amounts of energy, especially when compared to furnaces and air conditioners.

WATER HEATER

Try turning down the temperature. Over 140°F (60°C) is wasteful. A range of 115–120°F (46–50°C) is probably adequate. For reference, each 10°F or 5°C cuts energy use and your fuel bill for hot water by 13 percent.

Use the vacation setting when taking a trip. If you don't have this setting (look on the big red dial), turn the thermostat way down.

On older units, insulate the tank with a thermal blanket, available at hardware and home stores. Check the size of your unit before you go shopping.

If you need a new water heater, consider one of the newer tankless units. These save around 15 percent in "standby" energy losses from hot water sitting in the tank. And since there is no tank to rust out, they last a lifetime.

THE WASHER

Low-temperature washing saves lots of energy and money. Stay away from the hot-water cycle if at all possible, and always use the cold-water rinse. Warm-water washing is almost 50 percent more energy efficient and less costly than hot water. Cold-water efficiency versus hot water jumps up to a whopping 90 percent, saving you, on average, $120 per year.

Purchase products with multiple uses, like detergent with fabric softener or detergent with whiteners. And as mentioned previously, look for concentrated versions of both liquid and powdered detergents, as well as liquid fabric softeners.

Spots or stains? Try a prerinse stain remover rather than hot water.

Wash full loads or adjust the settings to use less water for smaller loads.

To conserve energy, try to place the machine as close as possible to the water heater. (Don't forget to insulate the pipe.)

THE DRYER

The dryer is a hidden energy and money eater in your home. In fact, drying clothes uses up to ten times more energy than washing them. Here are a few easy-to-follow ways to save:

Reduce the number of loads: Run full loads, but not too full, or the machine will not operate efficiently.

Clean lint out of the filter before using, and clean the vent from time to time.

Dry two or more loads in a row so that the second one benefits from the heat already in the machine.

Don't overdry clothes. Use the machine's moisture sensor, if it has one.

Try using the cool-down cycle, which uses heat already in the machine to finish drying garments.

Nice weather outside? Why not skip the dryer and hang-dry?

When you fold the laundry, keep a plastic bag handy for orphaned socks. After a few weeks, pull out and pair the ones that match. What's left is an instant ragbag, single socks and all.

ATTIC

Make sure the attic is well insulated. Much of the heat and cooling loss in your home goes through the roof, just as much of the heat loss in your body occurs through the top of your head!

Contact a cooling specialist to determine if an attic fan is worth considering. These units may help reduce the need for constant air conditioning.

General

Sooner or later, you will buy a new appliance or piece of furniture. What will you do with the old one?

Professor Michael Schiffer, a University of Arizona anthropologist and a colleague of William Rathje's, conducted an interview-survey of 184 households in Tucson, Arizona, to see what they did with the appliances they replaced. Over a five-year time span, the 184 households replaced 743 items, an average of 4 each! Of those items, 226 (30.5 percent) were kept at home. Another 253 (34.1 percent) were sold or given to reuse stores or strangers. A further 222 (29.9 percent) were given, sold, or loaned to relatives and friends. If you have been keeping track, you know that only 42 (5.6 percent) out of the 743 were thrown away! There are always young acquaintances, just starting out, who can use what you don't want any more.

While we're at home, we shouldn't forget the house itself. Because this structure is probably the most expensive and personal purchase anyone ever makes, general advice about what to buy is not easy to give. It is obvious, of course, that if you build from scratch in a newly opened area, you will generate tons of construction debris and cover much of your yard with stuff that is not natural to that environment. If you tear down an old structure and build a new one, according to a rule of thumb used by contractors, enough construction and demolition debris (C/D) will be discarded to fill up 40 percent of the volume of the completed house. Remodeling an existing structure to fit your individual needs is a great way to use less stuff—but even that will generate considerable C/D.

There is now an alternative method of home construction that is fast, incredibly sturdy, and made from 80 percent recycled materials. Even better, it creates virtually no C/D, and the finished house is affordable! This alternative method is called the Royal Building System. It was developed over the last ten years in Canada and has now been used to construct homes, schools, factories, motels, car washes, and townhouse complexes in more than 40 countries, including Japan, Canada, Russia, China, and the Philippines.

How quickly can a home be built? After the concrete foundation has set, three workmen can put up a basic 532 square foot two-bedroom in three days. How sturdy? Hollow panels and connectors simply slide together to form the walls and roof. Wall panels are then filled with concrete which is mechanically fastened to the foundation and roof. The result is a highly durable, virtually maintenance free, all-weather resistant and environmentally friendly structure, Houses built by Royal's system survived Hurricane Luis in the Caribbean and Supertyphoon Paka in the South Pacific without structural damage. Royal's buildings also withstand earthquakes and are waterproof. How is recycled plastic used? The building system utilizes Royal's patented technology to extrude a thin layer of virgin plastic onto the outside of the panel which incorporates recycled plastic on the hidden inner portions. Another Royal technology utilizes many different types of plastic waste, from HDPE to PP, to manufacture roof tiles which look like slate or cedar shakes. How much energy goes into heating and cooling? Initial studies show that the Royal system produces a structure that is noticeably less expensive to heat and cool than convential buildings.

How much C/D is created? Practically none at all, except for a few plastic sleeves around blocks of wiring. The building components, which are ready to assemble, are shipped in crates which are designed to be flattened, shipped back, and filled again.

How healthy are homes built from the Royal system? Testing has determined that airborne volatile organic compounds, which are frequently associated with adverse health reactions, occur at dramatically lower frequencies in a Royal structure than in a conventionally constructed building.

Not everyone will like the idea of living in a concrete house with a plastic skin, but the amazing variety of surface decorations and accessories in recycled plastic that mimic stone, brick, and the like are designed to give final products a customized look—and the price goes a long way toward making buyers feel at home. [For information, write to Royal Building Systems (CDN) Limited, 1 Royal Gate Blvd., Woodbridge, Ontario, Canada L4L 8Z7, or call Mark Badger at (905) 264-0701/fax (905) 264-0702, or call Angelo Bitondo (905) 264-0698/fax (905) 264-0699.]

Collections! Collect everything you can: train timetables, doilies, ashtrays, cigar boxes, Elvis memorabilia. . . . The 184 households Schiffer's students interviewed had 296 collections—a mean of 2.6 per household! All collections will appreciate in value if you can only find another like-minded collector. Just imagine how much stuff that keeps out of landfills!

There are still a bunch of other things you can do around the house:

Replace regular incandescent light bulbs with compact fluorescent bulbs, which last much longer and save energy as well.

Use curtains to keep out the sun in the summer and keep in the warmth in the winter.

If you have storm windows, use them. If you don't, consider buying them.

Make sure windows and doors don't leak air. Run a thin strip of paper around them. If it flutters, use weather stripping, caulk, and the like to close the leak.

Use turn-back thermostats, which allow you to turn down the heat or keep the air conditioner off when you're not usually home. This is especially helpful in winter, when you can sleep in cooler temperatures than are needed to keep you comfortable during the day. We suggest 56–62°F (14–17°C) at night and 66–72°F (19–22°C) during the day. These thermostats can help reduce your energy bill by up to 12 percent!

Before resorting to air-conditioning, try cross-ventilating by opening the top and bottom windows on opposite sides of the room. This should set up a nice, fresh breeze.

Clean the air filters in your window air conditioners. It'll take but a few minutes and save more than just a few dollars.

If you use a wood stove, clean the catalytic converter, if it has one. If it doesn't, get one!

If you use your fireplace(s) regularly, consider buying a

heat exchanger and glass doors. Doing so will turn the fireplace into an efficient heat source, rather than a major heat drain. (The exchanger channels heat into your home from the fireplace, and the glass doors keep heat in your home from escaping up the chimney.)

When not using a fireplace, close the doors or the flue to keep warm air from escaping up the chimney.

Turn out the lights when you leave the room, and close the doors to the outside.

Donate old clothes to the Salvation Army, Purple Heart, Red Cross, and so on. You might try selling clothes to a local thrift shop or to one of the chains of children's resale stores like Once Upon a Child or Children's Orchard.

Hold a garage sale. Give what's left to a charitable group.

Pets

We can't move on without discussing the 160 million pets walking, squawking, chirping, squeaking, swimming, and slithering around the house. All of our animal friends contribute to our household waste, some in mighty ways. For example, we estimate that cat litter alone accounts for about 1 percent, or 2 million tons, of annual garbage.

There are quite a few ways to cut pet-related wastes. Virtually all are both simple and money saving:

If you do not intend to become a professional breeder, have pets spayed or neutered. Call your vet, local Humane Society, animal league, or ASPCA chapter.

Try the newer cat litters that clump. You scoop out only what's been used, making the litter last longer.

Reuse old tennis balls, stuffed animals, or knotted socks as pet toys. Old towels make comfy bed liners.

Plastic deli containers make good water and food bowls. They also make great food scoops, as do gallon milk jugs cut along a diagonal.

Buy food and litter in bulk. Try to use dry, rather than moist, foods, and add your own water at home. You'll save money, store trips, and energy. Our figures show that bulk dry foods bought in paper or plastic bags reduce packaging waste by 75 percent versus moist foods bought in cans.

We could probably come up with a bunch more tips for home and hearth. We bet you can, too. Send them to us at *ULS Tips, Box 130116, Ann Arbor, MI 48113.* We'll use the best and most creative ideas in upcoming editions of *The ULS Report.* Who knows? If we get enough of them, we'll put them—along with appropriate identification of the innovator—in a sequel to this book!

FOOD

Do you know how much once-edible food you and your family waste each year? Probably not, since you don't pile it up in a corner or put it in a collection bin, as you do with your newspapers, cans, and bottles.

William Rathje is director of the Garbage Project at the University of Arizona. For twenty-five years Rathje's students have hand sorted scientifically collected samples of both fresh refuse put out for collection and older refuse dug out of landfills. According to Garbage Project records, the typical American household throws away between 10 and 15 percent of the food it purchases. That's enough to feed everyone in Canada, right down to the last Mountie and lumberjack. That represents fully 10 percent of all the garbage you throw out at home by weight. By the way, we're only talking about the edible stuff and not the debris—bones, peels, rinds, and so on. Food debris represents another 10 percent of household refuse. We're also understating these amounts, since the figures do not take into account food ground down the garbage disposal.

Looking at the entire solid-waste picture, food accounts for up to 7 percent of the garbage we send to landfills, meaning that we're wasting 14 million tons, or 28 billion pounds, of valuable resources. (That's 280 pounds per family per year—resources you've already paid for!) And as we stated previously, each bit of food thrown away also means we've wasted the water, agrochemicals, and energy needed to grow, transport, store, and sell it.

Because food is so important to us, the Garbage Project has been faithfully studying our consumption and disposal habits in great detail. And when it comes to discovering the truth, *garbage doesn't lie*. Here are some of the key pieces of learning gleaned from twenty-five years of rummaging through people's trash:

Fresh Produce

Fresh produce is wasted at ten times the rate of processed fruits and vegetables. The reason is simple. Processed foods usually don't spoil because we store them in the freezer or they are dried and kept in the refrigerator. They are basically ready-to-serve, with much of the preparation already done for us. When it comes to fresh produce, however, the clock is literally ticking, since spoilage is just around the corner. Also, there is much more preparation that needs to be done—peeling, pitting, chopping, grating, scooping, juicing, and coring, to name but a few. This finding has a few important implications:

- Processed produce can actually reduce waste. The key is to prepare only what will be eaten and to store what's left to be used again. (Keep a few rubber bands in the kitchen to use for reclosing polybags of fruits and vegetables.)
- Check your crisper and produce drawers *before* you shop so that you don't purchase fresh items that you already have on hand.
- Plan meals around items that will spoil quickly so that you use them up.
- Buy items you know your family will eat, like oranges, bananas, and apples. Save exotic fruits like kiwis and mangos for a try at a restaurant or a friend's house before taking the shopping plunge.
- Ditto for vegetables. Build your supplies from a core of veggies that are favorites.
- Prepare snack-type items in advance. If you want your kids to munch on carrots or celery, rather than candy, cut and chop them into small sticks when you bring the stuff home from the store. That way, when your children are hungry, the food is ready to be eaten, rather than ready to be cut up.

Food Shortages

Don't change your normal habits during a food shortage! If you do try something new, the chances are that you will end up wasting both more food and more money.

There was a widely publicized national "beef shortage" in the spring of 1973. Beef was hard to find and expensive. People bought cuts they weren't used to eating and didn't know how to prepare. They also bought large quantities (as a hedge against even higher prices) and didn't know how to store them properly. The result? While people complained bitterly about beef shortages and high prices, they wasted more beef than ever! Changing familiar behaviors led to waste.

The same thing happened in the "sugar shortage" in the spring of 1975. People tried new sweets with sugar substitutes and then threw out many of them. They stocked up on sugar products and tossed a lot away when chocolates developed light spots with age.

The lesson the Garbage Project learned was the "First Principle of Food Waste": *Foods that are used infrequently end up in the trash much more often than items that are eaten every day.* For example, sandwich bread and cold cereal are rarely wasted, but hot-dog buns and English muffins are thrown away at a much higher rate. Bread and cereal are used virtually every day. Specialty items, such as hot-dog buns or English muffins, are used once and then put in the fridge, where they are pushed to the side or back. By the time another specialty meal comes along, they may no longer be appetizing. In other words, buy multi-use products that can be used regularly (such as standard 12- or 24-ounce loaves of bread, which can be used at breakfast [toast], lunch [sandwiches], and dinner [just plain bread]), rather than specialty items designed for one particular purpose (such as hot-dog buns).

Once again, human nature rears its head: we are creatures of habit, and eat what we usually eat. We don't think much about other items, even if they're staring at us at eye level in the pantry or on the top shelf in the refrigerator. Sporadically used items may also require planning or preparation that we can't or won't do. For example, making a peanut butter sandwich on bread is easy—it's convenient and both ingredients are on hand in virtually every home. Preparing hot dogs isn't quite so simple—what if we only have the buns but not the franks? What if we're out of mustard or relish? What if we don't feel like cooking? Here are some tips for dealing with this situation:

- Familiarity breeds consumption. Buy what your family likes and will eat.
- Plan your meals in advance so that you buy ingredients for specific meals, rather than a bunch of items to fill up the fridge or pantry.
- Remember what home economists and dietitians always tell us: Don't shop when you're hungry. You're likely to buy anything just to feel as if there'll be plenty to eat.
- Stock up only on items that you can eat before they spoil. And remember that although the freezer is your

freshness friend, even subzero temperatures can't
keep food from ultimately spoiling or becoming damaged (freezer burn).

Everyone wants to try something different once in a
while. To cut waste, try it in threes. Find several specialty
uses for one item. Take sour cream—on baked potatoes
with chives (use the chives on salads as well and add them
to Mexican salsa and other dishes), in omelets with onions
and mushrooms, and on top of a large variety of Mexican
dishes, including burritos, chimichangas, and tostadas.

Processed Foods

*Households that purchase the highest proportion of
processed foods waste the highest percentage of fresh
foods.* Thus, the more processed foods a household
buys, the more likely it is to waste fresh meats, fruits, and
vegetables.

While this pattern seems odd, it does have a good expla-
nation, one we call "The Fast Lane Syndrome." Those
afflicted with the malady are very convenience oriented.
When they go to the store, they stock up on time-saving
processed items. But they feel guilty about doing so and
also buy fresh foods so that they can prepare healthy,
nutritious meals made from scratch. Unfortunately, they
never seem to have the time actually to make all the home-
cooked meals that they intended. At the end of the week,

the result is predictable—the garbage is filled with packaging from convenience foods as well as uneaten heads of lettuce and a host of other forlorn fresh fruits and vegetables.

If this pattern seems familiar to you, join the club. By now, our solution to this quandary shouldn't surprise you: *go with the flow.*

- If you only have time to prepare convenience foods, stick to them. You'll waste less than if you buy fresh stuff that never gets eaten. Remember that you can still reduce waste and save money by purchasing larger sizes of items such as peas or corn, buying items in bags rather than boxes, and sticking to items that your family will eat.
- Buy fresh foods in small quantities so that you're sure they'll be used up.
- When buying fresh meats and fish, keep in mind that the average person will eat only about a quarter of a pound. If you end up with more, cook only what you need now and freeze the rest. Label the foil or bag with the name of the item and the date when it was frozen. When putting it in the freezer, rotate your items so that the freshest ones are in the back and those that are closer to the end of their unnatural lives are easily seen and thus more likely to be prepared and eaten.

OK, you're buying smarter. What else can be done?

- Serve smaller portions and let people ask for seconds. Think how happy you'll be when kids ask for more! If they don't ask, you've begun to zero in on preparing the amount they will really eat.
- Serve meals in stages, to slow down eating speed. Serve salad first and wait a few minutes before bringing out the main course. Remember: your stomach fills up faster than your brain can tell you that your body is no longer hungry. By slowing down, you can better synchronize your eating habits with the amount of food you actually need. Once again, every slow meal will be a learning experience in source reduction . . . and perhaps weight reduction.
- Food for thought: substitute fruits, vegetables, and grains for meat, fish, and poultry. You'll reduce resource consumption, save money, and possibly be healthier and live longer: Even as far back as June 1961 the American Medical Association stated that a vegetarian diet can prevent up to 90 percent of strokes and 97 percent of heart attacks.
- Store leftovers carefully. Label them and put them in the front of the fridge so you're tempted to use them up.

Speaking of leftovers, there's an invaluable reference source available called *The Use It Up Cookbook: A Guide to Minimizing Food Waste* (self-published by Lois Carlson Willand, 145 Malcolm Ave. SE, Minneapolis, MN 55414, 612-378-9697). It's filled with very creative ways to use up common leftovers. Here are just a few things you can make with apples, besides sauce: Waldorf salad, fruit salad, stuffing, cake, and cream pie. How about applesauce bread, muffins, or even meatloaf?

The book includes a storage guide for perishable foods so that you can use them up before they spoil or go bad. For example, here are a few ways to get the most out of a few common vegetables:

- Asparagus—store unwashed, in plastic bags
- Carrots—remove tops, store in plastic bag or wrap
- Lettuce—wash and drain, place in bag or wrap
- Potatoes—store in cool, dark, dry place with good ventilation
- Green peas, lima beans—leave in pods
- Green beans—store in plastic bag or wrap
- Cucumbers—wash, dry, place in plastic bag or wrap

Learn a little about food safety. After any news report on the deadly disease bacillism transmitted in canned food, the Garbage Project often finds that people throw away unopened cans that have only been dented or slightly crushed during transport or stocking in the store. (The true sign of bacillism is an expanded or puffed-up can.) In twenty-five years of sorting household refuse, the Project has recorded only one unopened can that had expanded and was therefore likely to contain bacillism.

When cheese gets moldy, there is no need to throw all of it away. Cut off the mold and use the unaffected pieces.

Turn stale bread into salad croutons. For a more professional approach, try toasting the slices before cutting them up.

With any food, use your eyes and nose to check whether it's still edible. But don't take any chances. As the USDA says, when in doubt, throw it out!

One last reminder: always know why and how to prepare different types of food. The reason is best illustrated by a story: A woman is about to cook a ham. Her mother stops by for a visit. The cook cuts off the butt end of the ham and throws it out. "Why did you do that?" asks Mom. "Because you always did!" responds the cook. "Oh, dear," says Mom. "I only had a small pan, so I cut the butt off just to make the ham fit."

If, after all of this, you still have fruit and vegetable scraps, put them in the compost pile, rather than the garbage bin. If you live in an apartment or don't have a compost pile, you can still participate through *vermicomposting*—composting indoors with worms.

A good wormbox, made of a shallow plastic utility tub and filled with redworms, will do wonders with virtually all your food scraps, including eggshells (but NOT meat and bones). In fact, unless you have a very active compost pile outside, we'd suggest that worms are the best way to handle food waste. Simply keep the box under the sink or in the basement, but away from cats, who might be tempted to use it as a litterbox.

Worms eat the food, digest it, and excrete it in a form

politely referred to as castings. These are excellent soil conditioners and fertilizers and work well in your garden or as a dressing for houseplants. Castings are so nutritive they can even germinate avocado pits (another great way to reduce waste and beautify your home at the same time). Stick pits in the vermicomposting bin and forget about them for a month or two. When you see a tap root, transfer the pit to a pot and watch it grow.

Want to learn more? Pick up a copy of *Worms Eat My Garbage*, written by Mary Appelhof and published by Flower Press.

We have lots more tips on reducing food waste, especially during holiday time. We'll get to them in just a few chapters. But first, let's take a break and step outside.

THE GREAT OUTDOORS

We live in the land of plenty
but many things aren't plenty anymore . . .
let's leave some blue up above us
let's leave some green on the ground.
It's only ours to borrow
leave some for tomorrow.
Leave it and pass it on down.
—Alabama, "Pass It On Down"

There's at least as much to be done outside your home as in it. The reason is that about 15 percent, or 31 million tons, of all household trash is yard waste—grass clippings, leaves, hedge trimmings, and so forth. Yard wastes don't degrade in most landfills, and in most parts of the country they represent 20 percent or more of MSW. Because all this stuff is organic matter, there are far better ways to use it—ways that will help make your neighbors green with envy, your wallet green with cash, and the environment green with natural fertilizers and fewer polluting chemicals. All it takes is a little planning and systems thinking.

We also have a few novel ideas about using less when enjoying your outdoor surroundings. Whether it's a barbecue, picnic, or party, low-waste tips abound.

Composting

A compost pile is the key to maintaining a healthy lawn and garden. It will also help you eliminate virtually all outdoor waste, and it will save cash in the process. Contrary to popular belief, composting is easy and when done correctly, doesn't smell. You can start small with virtually no financial investment and work your way up to master composter, becoming the neighborhood Houdini of yard waste.

There are many excellent books written on composting, but in the spirit of using less, we've distilled much of the advice down to a few easy-to-understand paragraphs:

First, wait until the weather is consistently warm. Choose a spot away from wooden structures including homes, garages, and fences. You will want a spot with good drainage, but near enough to a hose that the pile can be moistened if necessary.

A simple 3'×3'×3' pile will do. Cover it with plastic when it rains to keep it from getting drenched. (Waterlogged piles are the ones that smell so bad!) If you prefer an enclosed composter, there are many good ones on the market, including a few made from 100 percent recycled polyethylene or other plastics. Call your local municipal waste management department before you go shopping, since many towns will provide you with composters at very attractive prices.

Next, keep in mind what you can and cannot put in the pile. Leaves, grass clippings, and small branches are great, but stay away from any sticks and weeds that have gone to seed, diseased plants, or pesticide-treated material. Fruits, vegetables, husks, skins, and peels are also good, as is brown kraft paper. DO NOT include meats, dairy products or eggs, as these will attract all sorts of nasty things like flies, maggots, and hungry animals. Also stay away from cat litter, coal or charcoal ashes (wood ashes are OK), or glossy paper.

Now it's time to stockpile the materials—outside the bin if you're using one. The first step is to divide items into brown (carbon rich) and green (nitrogen rich) piles. Brown items include straw, dried leaves, wood chips, kraft paper, and pine cones or needles. Green items include grass clippings, fresh leaves, and hedge trimmings. It's very important that your finished pile be about 95 percent brown stuff and 5 percent green stuff, so go easy on collecting grass clippings. (We'll tell you how in a few minutes.) Too much of the green, nitrogen-bearing material will make the pile odiferous and slow down the degradation process.

You will also need a starter, which performs a similar function to yeast when making bread. Old compost will do.

Since you probably don't have any around, ask a neighbor; or you can always get bagged compost at a garden store, or bagged manure, if you prefer.

Now, start layering the green and brown piles into a new pile. After you put down a layer of brown, sprinkle on some of the starter and water so that it's moist, not soaked. Do the same with the green stuff, being careful to keep green layers much thinner than brown ones.

Finally, fork the layers into the bin, mixing as you go. Blend well, and water as necessary to make sure the entire pile is moist but not soggy. Add table scraps now, or over the next few weeks.

One more thing: aeration is critical. Recent studies indicate that the old method of aerating by continually turning the pile doesn't work as well as a continuous ventilation process. Use a dowel or broom handle to poke the pile from top to bottom in a number of places. This will set up convection currents that do the work for you. Another way to aerate is to punch holes along the length of a number of pieces of plastic piping and insert the pipes into the pile, horizontally or vertically. Better yet, insert the pipes as you are mixing in the brown and green portions of the heap.

Active composting should begin within 48 hours. The pile will cook by itself, with temperatures in the 120° to 150°F range. Stir once a week and add water as necessary to keep moist.

You'll soon see steam rising, indicating an active pile. In about three weeks, the steam will stop and the pile will cool. Contents will be brown and crumbly. It's time to put your newly made compost to work in the beds and the lawn.

Lawns

If you have a large yard, buy a mulching mower, which chops the clippings into very small pieces that stay on the lawn instead of being raked up or bagged. There are many advantages:

- There's nothing to throw away.
- Mulch acts as fertilizer, keeping your lawn thick and healthy.
- Since you fertilize less, you save money and reduce the amount of chemicals that can seep into the groundwater and aquifers.
- You save time, since there's nothing to rake and fewer fertilizing occasions.

If you have a very small yard, consider a person-powered reel-to-reel mower. If this is impractical, consider an electric mower. It's quieter and cleaner than gas-powered models. Also, any pollution created by fuel use occurs at the power plant, which is tightly regulated for emissions. The same can't be said for gas mowers, which emit pollution individually and uncontrollably. (In fact, we think we remember an EPA study a few years back indicating that mowers were worse polluters than cars!)

Whatever type of mower you have, tune it up and clean it. Kits with spark plugs and air filters that fit your mower are readily available at lawn-care stores.

When changing the oil, recycle it or make sure you are disposing of it in the proper manner. Check with your city's sanitation department for proper procedures.

Sharpen the blade with a file, rather than replace it.

Reduce the amount of area covered by grass. This will cut back on the amount of lawn to be mowed, as well as the quantity of fertilizers and weed killers needed to keep grass healthy. Put beds of ground cover such as pachysandra, vinca, or English ivy around trees. This is good for the trees, too, since you won't have to mow as closely, and trees are less likely to be whacked by the mower or its blades.

Check all hoses, couplings, and faucets for leaks and fix as necessary.

Adjust sprinklers as appropriate so that you don't water the street, sidewalk, or house.

If you have an automatic sprinkler system, check that the heads are clean, in proper working order, and unobstructed by stones or fallen branches. We've seen too many sprinklers aimed permanently at passing cars, rather than at thirsty plants.

Water in the early morning or evening, not during the heat of the day. This way, water will soak into the ground, rather than simply evaporate into the air.

Use timers to ensure that lawns aren't overwatered.

Aerate the lawn to increase water penetration. You can

rent an aerating device from most equipment rental companies.

Put that compost to good use. According to *Smart Yard*, you can put down 250 pounds of compost per 100 square feet of sandy soil, 500 pounds on loamy soil, and 1,200 pounds on clay soil. Now that's a LOT of compost!

Avoid overfertilizing, which increases the demand for water.

Consider using organic fertilizers. They may cost a little more to buy, but you'll need fewer feedings and won't be contributing to local groundwater pollution problems.

Plan lawns around local conditions. Imported grasses and plants may require too much water or fertilizer to maintain in your type of surroundings.

Controlling weeds helps reduce water consumption. The best thing to do is to prevent weeds from growing. To do so, use a crabgrass "pre-emergent" in the early spring. Pre-emergents cover bare spots and prevent weeds from getting a toehold in your lawn.

Gardens

One of the best ways to reduce waste is by sticking to plants that are easy to cultivate in your area. For example, melons don't do well in the North, as cool August nights and early frosts seriously reduce the chances of a ripe crop.

As with grasses, stick to local plant species. Even if foreign varieties do well, they may end up doing *too* well. Plants with no natural enemies can thrive to the point where they begin displacing local species, creating all sorts of problems. (Just ask your friends in the South about kudzu!)

Also, if plants call for bright sun, don't expect that they'll do well in the shade. Many tomato crops have been wasted by suburban farmers who hoped that a little shade would be all right. The same works in reverse—many an impatiens bed has shown less than optimal results when planted in too much sun.

Nonporous glazed and ceramic pots reduce water evaporation. Use them for outside and inside plants.

It is very important to protect young seedlings. Shelter them by covering with paper bags or, for a see-through shelter, slice the bottoms off plastic milk jugs and place the jugs over tiny plants. Cut the bottoms into strips and use as markers. Recycle when you're done.

Save old seeds. According to *Garden Answers*, the life expectancy of many common seeds is quite long, such as beans (3 years), cucumber (5 years), lettuce (6 years), and peppers (2 years).

Grow vegetables your family will eat. A bumper crop of zucchini may be pretty to look at and make you feel good, but if it's not eaten, it'll just go to waste.

Reduce water use by covering beds with lots of compost or mulch. Use soaker hoses and drip systems, rather than sprinklers. Also, try to create level beds, eliminating water runoff.

Reduce weeds by (1) seeding heavily; (2) looking for plants that block weed growth by sprouting early, quickly, and producing large leaves or numerous branches; and (3) weeding when the ground is wet so the roots pull out easily. This last point is especially helpful for removing weeds with very deep taproots, such as dandelions and pigweed.

Use compost or mulch around shrubs, trees, and vegetables to hold in moisture and keep out weeds.

Look for simple and effective ways to reduce the use of harsh or hazardous chemicals. For example, one way to cut down on the need for fungicides is to keep from overwatering. Before using insecticides, try spraying aphids and other garden pests with soapy water. If you have problems with slugs or snails, put out a pan of something naturally attractive to them, like white vinegar or beer.

Pools, Decks, and Spas

If you have a pool or spa, buy and use a cover. It will retain heat and reduce water loss by 90 percent.

Try turning the heat down a bit or doing with a little less water. (This may be one of the biggest energy-saving tips in this book: a pool heater uses as much energy as ten gas or electric barbecue grills.)

If you have pool lights, make sure they're turned off when the pool is not in use, or put them on timers.

Building a deck? Consider plastic lumber made from recycled materials. It won't warp or rot and is not very tasty to bugs. Plastic lumber is also much cheaper to buy and maintain than traditional deck woods such as cedar. Other benefits include the fact that it's not made from virgin materials and does not need to be stained often or sealed at all; also, there are no splinters to invade bare feet.

Consider using plastic lumber to replace old railroad ties you may be using for decorative planters, terraces, and steps, as well.

Forget about bug zappers. They use a lot of electricity, tend to bring bugs into the area, and kill a source of food for birds, spiders, and other beneficial creatures. Try a citronella candle; instead of attracting mosquitoes, it repels them.

Barbecues

Americans love cookouts. In fact, they are the single most popular form of home entertaining. Here are a few ways to have fun and use less:

If you have a gas grill, change your cleaning habits. Instead of keeping the fire going after you cook so you can burn off residue, save gas by turning off the grill. Clean up at the next use—after warm-up, but before cooking. Use a wire brush. No harsh cleaners are necessary; you save gas and the cost of cleaners.

No matter what type of grill you have, save indoor energy by keeping the oven off and cooking the entire meal on the barbie. Wrap vegetables in foil and grill them. Soak corn on the cob in the husk in water and then steam on the grill. Poach fish fillets quickly and easily by wrapping in foil with a little white wine and butter, then placing on the hot grill for about five minutes.

Turn the heat down, rather than raise the grill up and away from the coals. This is especially helpful for gas and electric barbecue energy savings.

Cooking for only a few? Try using just one side of the grill if you have a double-burner setup.

Cook only what you need. Most guests will eat just one or two of anything—corn, burgers, hot dogs, and so on.

Hint to charcoal users: When done cooking, smother the coals by closing the vents and putting the lid on. You can use the leftover coals to start the next fire, saving on charcoal.

If using disposable cups and plates, leave a few magic markers around so that guests can label their possessions. This will cut way down on the number used per person, since it'll be obvious whose is whose.

Reuse plastic containers and reduce food waste by filling them with leftover potato salad, cole slaw, and the like, and giving them to guests to take home.

Picnics

The trick here is to figure out how to leave behind the least amount of waste. Again, the key is to plan ahead:

If multiple families are attending, try to carpool to the picnic site.

Pack food in reusable containers and bags.

Put drinks in thermos bottles, or reuse glass and plastic bottles.

After packing the cooler, fill clean plastic grocery bags with ice. Put the bags on top of the food to keep it cool. Use the ice in your drinks, and the bags for garbage. Save one bag for compostable items like fruit peels and vegetable stems. Bring them home and compost.

Roll used aluminum foil in a ball. Bring it home to reuse or recycle.

See what can be done with a little planning? Your compost pile alone will eliminate much of your yard waste, reduce both water and fertilizer usage and costs, while making your lawn and garden a happier and healthier place to be. Add in the energy you saved, and you've definitely caught the ULS bug. Now it's time to leave the world of recreation and leisure and take a look at what can be done at work and school.

WORK AND
SCHOOL

*She has submitted a large report [on how to decrease garbage
production] to authorities at LAX [Los Angeles International
Airport]. And she feels sort of guilty about it—production of the
300-page main report (two copies), plus the 50-page "Executive
Analysis" (100 copies)—[produced] nearly 6,000 pages in all.*
—Los Angeles Times Magazine
describing a waste audit by Ellen Hae

It's a blizzard! Of paper, that is. The rise of the service
economy over the past thirty-five or so years has also given
rise to the paper economy. Both were aided by a revolu-
tion in widely used office equipment: computers, printers,
copiers, and fax machines.

Today, office paper and other business-related materials (brochures, flyers, newsletters, pamphlets) represent
the largest source of nondurable solid waste, bigger than
such typically vilified items as disposable diapers or plastic
packaging. For perspective, the volume of office paper

and commercial printing increased a whopping 245 percent between 1960 and 1994, from 3.9 million to 13.5 million tons. During this time, the increase in all other municipal solid waste generated was much less—about 133 percent (which is still a lot!).

And even though much of this paper, especially the stuff spewed out of printers and copiers, is of high quality and easily recycled, we're sending memos at a much faster rate than can be dealt with by recycling programs. Whatever happened to the so-called paperless society?

At school, the situation is similar. Lots of memos, worksheets, note paper, artwork, signs, banners, and so on. There's also the cafeteria, a major source of school-based waste.

Unlike trash collection at most homes, businesses and schools pay to have stuff hauled away, usually by the Dumpster-full. So by using less and reducing the number of Dumpster loads, the environment will benefit, but so, too, will the bottom line at work and the budget at school.

At Work

When it comes to paper, the office is the perfect place to learn how to reduce, reuse, and recycle, in that order. That's because up to 80 percent of office waste is high-grade white paper. By creating a system that follows the three Rs, it's possible to eliminate virtually ALL paper waste. We know—the only paper at one of our offices that doesn't get recycled is high-gloss advertising materials that we have little control over. We estimate that since starting our tree-saving program, waste from office paper has been reduced an amazing 99 percent! Here's what to do:

REDUCE

Try to go paperless as much as possible. Instead of writing separate memos, share electronic files, voice mail, and e-mail with associates. Save what you need electronically; print out only what you'll need as hard copy. If you must send paper to more than one person, attach a routing slip and pass along as necessary. Do the same with newspaper and magazine subscriptions.

If your company has electronic-funds transfer for payroll, select this option. If your company doesn't have electronic transfer, work to have a system set up. Just as critical, work with suppliers and vendors to arrange for electronic-funds transfer between firms.

Reduce fax traffic by switching to fax modems. You can send and receive faxes on your computer and view them on screen. For those worth saving, do so electronically.

Try to skip cover sheets when sending faxes. Most letters and memos already include the name of the receiver, and your fax machine probably stamps your name and phone number on the top of each page anyway.

Reduce the weight of the paper used in your printers, copiers, and fax machines. Given how much paper the typical office uses in a year, even a few ounces saved per ream adds up quickly, both financially and environmentally.

Photocopy on both sides of the paper. The extra few seconds it takes to push the "duplex," or "double-sided," button on the machine can help cut copy paper usage by almost as much as 50 percent.

Reduce the amount of paper that is easily available. Psychologically, when people go to the supply closet and see ream upon ream of paper, they think that paper is plentiful and cheap. But when they see less and are led to believe that there isn't any more, or that additional quantities will cost more and be charged to their budget, paper consumption will drop dramatically! (Ditto for pencils, pens, clips, rubber bands, erasers, and other supplies.)

REUSE

Flip faxes over and use the paper again. If you want your faxes printed, get a "plain paper" versus a "thermal" fax. Thermal paper is harder to write on, discolors, and can't be reused or recycled.

Collate old single-sided memos, faxes, and the like into piles, with the printed side facedown. Separate them into piles of about twenty-five sheets. Staple each pile four times along the edge of one of the two longer sides. Use the paper cutter to divide the stapled pile into two stapled sections, creating 5.5″ × 8.5″ scratch pads.

When all the name and address spaces on interoffice

mail envelopes have been filled in, tape a blank piece of paper to the envelope and label with two columns, one for name and the other for address. (Better yet, have your art department develop a form.) Voila! The envelope can be used again and again!

Keep a large plastic bag next to the shredder, and fill it when the shredder basket becomes full. Use this material for packaging cushioning, eliminating the need to purchase "peanuts." (Check with your mail-room to see if they can use it, too.)

RECYCLE

Clearly mark recycling bins and provide an incentive for using them. A simple thing to do is to credit sections or departments for part of the money that the company receives when it sells the paper. (Ask your purchasing or maintenance department how much it is paid per pound of recycled paper. Weigh a full recycling bin to find out what it is worth and negotiate a credit. Use the money for employee perks, such as a party, charitable donation, or whatever employees would like to work toward.)

Remove all sticky notes from paper headed for the recycling bin. These little devils may be convenient, but they can ruin an entire batch of recyclable paper, forcing the mill to throw it all away. (Use the scratch-paper idea described above to replace sticky notes and attach with reusable paper clips.)

Buy and use white paper as much as possible. If you need colors, try to purchase light ones; they use less dye and are easier to recycle. Use the cardboard backs of paper tablets as dividers in your file drawers.

OTHER TIPS

Switch to refillable pens and mechanical pencils. Long term, this will save money along with reducing a good deal of waste.

Encourage employee carpooling. Consider charging for parking space, or offer an incentive to those people who carpool regularly. Some organizations even provide vans for employees to use, splitting the cost of the van among the users and subsidizing part of the expenses. Thus, the cost to carpool or use a van is less than the cost of driving alone. Gas usage will drop, too.

Have your maintenance department or local utility company do an energy audit, looking for ways to cut electricity usage. Switching to more efficient overhead lights, reducing office temperature slightly, and installing skylights are all possible sources for savings.

Join the EPA's Waste Wise (800-EPA-WISE) and Green Lights (888-STAR-YES) programs, which can provide savings tips and help you set and achieve conservation and cost-reduction goals. Waste Wise examines all phases of your business, while Green Lights focuses (obviously) on lighting, especially the use of fluorescent fixtures, bulbs, and reflectors.

Install long-lasting compact fluorescent bulbs in exit

signs and other fixtures that are left on for long periods of time.

Turn off all lights and equipment (other than fax machines) at night. Make sure all thermostats can be turned down after work as well.

When purchasing new equipment, look for the EPA's "Energy Star" logo, which means the unit is an energy-efficient one. Also, have technical support folks make sure that all computers, monitors, and printers that have Energy Star capabilities are actually using them.

Setting up a home office? Check out the new multi-function machines that combine a laser printer, fax, scanner, and copier. You'll not only reduce the amount of equipment you own, you'll save significant money as well as valuable office space.

For laser printers, remanufactured cartridges can save 40 to 50 percent over buying new. To save money and the environment, invest in and maintain a photo-copy machine that produces good copies—there's no good reason to waste paper.

When comparison shopping for electronics equipment, consider the length of warranties. Twice in the last year one of the authors had major problems with a three-year-old computer. The first reaction both times was to buy a new one. But by checking the warranty, it was determined that both problems would be fixed for free, saving a lot of money and keeping a machine out of the trash.

A good strategy when purchasing new computer equipment is to buy units that are easy to upgrade. We have successfully kept up with increases in processor speed merely by replacing a board, rather than the entire computer. We were even able to sell the old boards to people who wished to upgrade their even older machines!

At School

Obviously, the same tactics mentioned above apply at school. There are a few more things that can be done to help reduce the flow of paper toward the waste stream:

If you send newsletters or other materials home through the mail, try to eliminate envelopes. Simply fold, staple, address, and post.

Many, if not most, schools have Internet access. Instead of sending home announcements or calendars to students with home Internet access, put the information up on the school's Web site. Do the same with assignment sheets.

Even with the Internet, schools are still volcanoes that constantly spew out tons of paper. Not surprisingly, high schools produce far more white ledger paper than middle or elementary school. This most recyclable of papers accounts for about 20 percent of the total waste stream in high schools that the Garbage Project has studied. Ask students to buy two-sided notebook paper and to use it.

Also ask them to buy recycled paper, and, of course, to recycle their schoolwork.

Give the students the responsibility of setting up and maintaining collection boxes, storing the paper for pickup, and even negotiating rates of pay with a wastepaper dealer or garbage hauler. That way, they'll learn both the environmental benefits and the economic realities of recycling firsthand.

Many schools have used recycling to benefit their communities in other ways. One Flagstaff, Arizona, junior high school's recycling program is staffed and run by the Trainable Mentally Handicapped Students. They earn between $3 and $7 weekly and contribute it to their community-based instruction program that helps them develop survival skills for daily living. Besides providing money for their special education needs, the recycling program also helps the students develop self-esteem and a sense of accomplishment. Several schools in Phoenix, Arizona, are involved in a joint partnership with the city of Phoenix and the Arizona Center for the Blind and Visually Impaired, Inc. Each classroom sorts its white and mixed-color paper scraps, which are collected bimonthly by Student Council members and placed in barrels for pickup every two weeks. The city of Phoenix collects the paper and delivers it to the Arizona Center for the Blind and Visually Impaired, where it is recycled. Recycling profits support programs for that center. In return, the Center offers field trips to Phoenix students through their recycling plant.

THE CAFETERIA

Besides paper, the other major source of waste is in the cafeteria. Between lunches brought from home and food left over from the serving line, there's plenty of stuff heading to the landfill that can be avoided. Perhaps not surprisingly, the Garbage Project found that the most food is wasted in the lower grades: 30 percent of the waste stream from elementary schools is typically food waste, 27 percent from middle schools, and 17 percent from high schools.

Not much of this waste is preparation debris, because most food services in schools buy "ready-to-use" produce. It is more labor efficient and generates no skins, leaves, or peels to go into the garbage. That means that the food waste is real "waste"—something that was ready to eat, but wasn't eaten. One reason for the high waste in elementary schools is that all the students are usually served one basic set meal, without much real choice. The response to this problem has been a program called "offer vs. serve." Instead of "serving" a set meal, school cafeterias "offer" students the choice of three or four food items. A scientific hands-on study that compared "offer" to "serve" waste demonstrated that choices have reduced food waste, saved money, and reduced the labors of the kitchen staff.

Studies of food waste in schools found that there was a great deal of waste in the lunches brought from home. The key to decreasing that waste, once again, is to look at the whole picture and plan accordingly. If students bring lunch to school, here are six simple things to do:

- Start with a reusable lunch box. Metal ones are very sturdy, while plastic ones are easy to clean and are rustproof. Fabric sacks are also a possibility, but get dirty easily and are harder to rinse off.

- Reuse plastic and paper bags from stores rather than buy paper lunch sacks.
- Now is not the time to try giving kids something new or exotic. Chances are, it will end up in the garbage. Stick to what you know is good for your children and what they will eat. Experiment at home before sending items to school.
- Put sandwiches, cookies, carrots, and celery in reusable containers such as Tupperware-type containers or Ziploc bags. (Remind students to put these back in the box or bag and bring them home to be reused.)
- Pack fresh fruit, since most types don't need any additional packaging.
- Buy liquids in concentrated form. Use a glass or plastic bottle you have on hand to prepare and store the juice. Pour into a thermos-type container that fits in the lunch box. Rubbermaid even sells a reusable plastic juice container the same size as disposable "juice boxes."

To reduce trash from both hot lunches prepared at school and packed lunches from home, we've gleaned some great ideas from waste experts around the country. These should be of use to school personnel:

- Have the serving staff practice portion control so that less food goes in the trash.

- If you serve drinks in disposable cups, try to eliminate straws and lids.
- Suggest that different classes conduct studies of food waste at school throughout the year. If they carefully sort and weigh the foods wasted, they will learn lessons about scientific methods and about resource waste at the same time. Be sure to go through the trash cans in the halls, classrooms, and outside the building. Kids are constantly buying snacks. The sorters will be shocked at how much of that impulse buying goes to waste. (They will also be surprised at how many lunches brought from home are thrown out untouched!) Over time, you should know what kids will and will not eat and be able to save considerable food from being wasted and perhaps be able to reduce your cafeteria expenditures.
- Look into starting a compost program so that leftovers like fruit and vegetable scraps can be turned back into something valuable: mulch for the school's lawn and garden areas. (Don't forget to include paper bags left from home-prepared lunches.) There are a number of reasonably inexpensive containers designed for school-size composting, and some are even made from recycled plastic.
- Work with local co-ops and farmers to buy produce locally. It will generally be fresher, so it creates less spoilage and waste. Since it will be transported only over short distances, odds are that a great deal of packaging can be eliminated and/or returned for reuse.

- Talk to local recycling agencies about recycling items such as metal cans and glass bottles, plastic and paper milk cartons, juice boxes, and the omnipresent and very recyclable corrugated cardboard boxes in which so much food and so many food containers are delivered to the school.
- If milk at school is served in paperboard cartons that aren't being recycled, consider switching to flexible mini-sip pouches. These produce much less waste and are far easier to compact.
- Build an aluminum-foil ball. Have kids clean and reuse whatever foil they have brought to school to build the biggest possible ball. Your local recycling organizations should be quite pleased to be able to take away so much clean material at one time and in one piece.
- Contact local food-gathering organizations, including Foodchain and Second Harvest, to determine if left-over food can be picked up and donated to shelters, food banks, etc.
- Throw a party! Use some of the financial savings from reduced food expenditures or trash collections to reward students for their efforts. (We'll leave it up to you to determine how to make the celebration a low-waste one.)

A FEW MORE IDEAS

If your school is like most, the end of the year is the time when the lost and found is overflowing and all sorts of odds and ends turn up. Rather than throw all this stuff away, hold a sale or have the PTA do so as a fund raiser. As the saying goes, one person's old shirt is another person's new one. Consider donating old textbooks as well. You'd be amazed how interesting they can be to someone who doesn't *have* to read them for a test!

Don't forget about bathrooms. Post signs reminding students to turn off the water when they're done washing their hands, and to take only the amount of paper toweling they need. Many paper towel dispensers have three different settings: large, medium, and small. It may be possible to adjust the feed of towels to the needs of different-size students. Also, consider converting to air-drying machines, thus eliminating paper towels completely.

And don't forget about school buses. Because they usually occur in fleets, there are lots of ways to cut down on wastes, some of them hazardous, and to cut down on expenses:

- Buy reusable air filters that can be cleaned and replaced three or four times.
- Rebuild old radiators, rather than buy new ones.
- Recycle used motor oil.
- Recap or retread tires. If the sidewalls stay strong, this can be done twice. The only caution is that, for safety's sake, recaps and retreads can be used only on the back axles of school buses.
- Legal requirements prohibit the release of Freon into the air. School districts can reuse Freon from bus air conditioners and from cooling units in buildings. Cer-

tified personnel remove the Freon using a Freon recapture machine that can also recharge the Freon.

Have teachers bring in their own mugs for use in the teacher's lounge.

If you need more playground equipment, ask parents for donations of items like balls and bats. Many people have a few of these things lying around their house, unused since their kids outgrew them.

Hold a used-book sale to benefit the school. Have students and parents donate unwanted books in good condition. Whatever is left after the sale can be returned, turned over to a used book or thrift shop, or used to fill in the school library.

At the college and university level there is one additional plan you can implement. Every spring, during exams, students are madly packing up to go home or on vacation or even to another institution for summer school. They have usually collected a lot more appliances, furniture, knickknacks, clothes, and shoes than they have room for in a car or on a plane. Most of the stuff they can't carry winds up in the garbage, even though it is perfectly usable.

Why not find an open area in a dorm parking lot or some other space convenient to student housing and start an impromptu waste exchange? There are plenty of people who could use the appliances and additional items that would otherwise be tossed out. If you can find cheap storage for over the summer, you might even be able to sell what was not exchanged or given away and make a little cash when the students come back in the fall. It just takes someone to bring people together to exchange stuff, rather than buy and waste more of it.

Let's move on to the times when we leave school and work behind—travel and vacations.

ON THE ROAD

Oh, Lord, Mr. Ford, how I wish that you could see,
What your simple horseless carriage has become.
It seems your contribution to man, to say the least,
got a little out of hand.
Oh, Lord, Mr. Ford, what have you done!
—Jerry Reed, "Oh, Lord, Mr. Ford"

As the saying goes, life is a journey. And all journeys, no matter how short or how long, require energy to get you from here to there. Thousands of years ago, we relied on such renewable resources as bananas, nuts, lettuce, fish, and bison meat to supply the energy we needed to travel. Today, we still need these things, but because we tend to go so much farther, we have come to rely on one particular nonrenewable energy resource as well: gasoline.

The main environmental problem with gasoline, quite frankly, isn't that we are running out of it—no one knows for sure when or if this will happen—but that it produces so much carbon dioxide. And as we have already mentioned, increases in carbon dioxide production are considered to be a key factor behind the buildup of greenhouse gases in the atmosphere.

To get a handle on how much CO_2 is produced by your car, consider that a gallon of gasoline weighs about 8 pounds. When the gas is burned, the carbon reacts with oxygen from the air to produce carbon dioxide. The result is *about 22 pounds of CO_2 produced per each gallon of gasoline burned.* Let's assume your driving habits are average, around 11,800 miles a year, at about 20 miles per gallon. This means you use 590 gallons of gas annually, and create 13,000 pounds, or 6.5 tons, of CO_2!

Now, let's look at how much carbon dioxide we all produce. Considering that we burn about 150 billion gallons of gasoline in this country each year, we're talking about 3.3 trillion pounds, or 1.6 billion tons, of carbon dioxide produced by motor vehicles each year in the United States alone. In terms of waste, annual carbon dioxide production is eight times the size of our annual municipal solid-waste production!

Unfortunately, we are doing everything we can to use as much gasoline as we possibly can. As shown in table 10.1, we are not only driving more cars and trucks but we are driving them farther and faster. All three factors contribute to increases in gasoline consumption. Along with these trends is the fact that our fairly recent love affair with sport-utility vehicles is pushing us toward even larger and more inefficient engines, which get fewer miles per gallon. This, too, is increasing our level of gasoline consumption.

TABLE 10.1

HIGHWAY HEADACHES

	1980	1994	PERCENT CHANGE
Cars in use (millions)	105	122	16.2
Trucks in use (millions)	35	71	100.2
Miles driven per car annually	9,100	11,800	29.0
Average highway speed (mph)	58	61	5.2

Sources: U.S. Federal Highway Administration, American Automobile Manufacturers Association.

There are other problems associated with cars as well. The Rubber Manufacturers Association reports that we replace about 200 million tires annually, which means that we also throw almost that many away. The major problem is that because of the hollow inner tube, tires float to the surface of landfills, are collected into huge piles, and then catch and hold standing water, which breeds mosquitoes. Even worse, these piles can catch on fire! In addition, *Consumer Reports* estimates that each year, more than 170 million gallons of used motor oil are disposed of improperly in sewers and backyards by do-it-yourselfers. For reference, 1 gallon of used oil in fresh water renders 1 million gallons undrinkable.

You'll notice that all of the things we've talked about are

the result of driving, not of owning the car itself. It turns out that about 90 percent of the environmental damage caused by automobiles is related to usage, not production. This means that while recycling automobile components at the junkyard may be a valuable thing to do, using less gas—driving less—and preventing waste is Environmental Job One.

Once again, a good dose of common sense and an eye toward saving money will go a long way in the fight to reduce the impact of automobile usage. Here's what you can do to help:

Alternative Transportation

If you live close to work, why not walk or ride a bike?

Give public transportation a try. Check with your company to see if they provide incentives for doing so. If not, your local transportation authority may be able to help in this regard.

Try to set up a car pool or get a group together in a van. There's a great little booklet available called *The Joy of Carpooling* that can help. To receive a copy, send $3 along with a double-stamped #10 envelope to Susan Shankle, The Joy of Carpooling, 3182 Campus Dr. #364, San Mateo, CA 94403.

Routine Maintenance

Keeping a car in good running order will maintain efficiency *and* make it last longer. You'll save on repairs in the long run and end up buying fewer cars as well. Here's what to do:

Regularly check your tires to determine if they are inflated correctly. This will save on wear and tear and help you achieve maximum fuel efficiency.

Rotate and balance tires as called for in your owner's manual. Tires will last longer, saving you cash by reducing the frequency of buying a new set. Many stores will rotate tires for free, if you bought them there.

Get regular tune-ups and oil changes. Both will help maintain efficiency and long life, while reducing the need for expensive repairs.

If you change your own oil, dispose of it properly. Check with your town's solid-waste division to receive proper instructions and information on waste-oil recycling programs.

Wash off salt and dirt, touch up scratches, then wax and seal. A clean machine is a long-lasting machine.

Have the heating and cooling system inspected in the fall and spring, respectively. If not operating efficiently, climate controls can waste significant fuel.

Driving Tips

Avoid quick stops and starts, as these take their toll on engine and brake life.

After about 45 miles per hour, fuel efficiency drops off dramatically, so try not to drive too fast or over long distances when you can avoid it.

When approaching a red light, slow down sooner, so that you don't always have to apply the brakes. This will save on brake wear, and it may be a safer way to stop. Also, if the light happens to turn green before you've come to a complete stop, you can more easily get back up to speed faster, saving on fuel.

If it's hot outside, use the air conditioner. Today's more aerodynamic cars are designed to be driven with the windows closed. Using the AC burns less fuel than does overcoming the increased drag created by open windows.

If it's cold out, warm up the car for a few minutes. Most of the pollution caused by cars occurs in the first few minutes, before the engine and catalytic converter are operating efficiently. If it's especially cold, it takes a while for the oil to warm up, thin out, and do its job correctly. Waiting that extra minute will thus keep smog out of the air, and keep your auto out of the repair shop.

If stopping for more than a minute or so, turn the ignition off. It takes less energy to turn the ignition on than to keep the crankshaft turning.

Planning

Consolidate trips. If you're going to the west side of town, think about everything you can do while over there: hit the post office, bank, and dry cleaner all in one trip, rather than in separate journeys.

Shop where you live. You'll be supporting the local economy and the local environment.

When buying a new car, comparison-shop based on fuel efficiency, along with other needed features. Saving a few miles per gallon can really add up. For example, over its 120,000-mile life, a car that gets 23 miles per gallon will ultimately use 780 gallons less than a similar model that only gets 20 miles per gallon. That's a savings of about $1,000, enough for about three free monthly loan payments.

Be practical when you purchase a new vehicle. If you have a small family and don't plan on going on safari or visiting the Arctic Circle, you probably don't need a gas-guzzling sport-utility vehicle. If you live in areas with lots of snow or mud that make ownership a practical matter, remember to switch to 2-wheel drive on clear days.

Cars and gasoline aren't the only areas where we can watch our waste when traveling. There are plenty of simple things we can do on the plane or train and in the hotels, motels, campsites, theme parks, and restaurants where we will be hanging out:

Before Leaving Home

Turn down the heat or turn off the air-conditioning. Also remember to turn the hot-water heater to its "Vacation" setting.

Unplug appliances such as TVs, cable boxes, and computers. This will protect them in the event of storms or power surges in your absence and save you money, since many of these devices draw power continuously.

If you have a water bed, lower the heater temperature by 10 degrees.

Stop the newspaper. Many papers will donate your unused copies to local schools, libraries, and other worthy institutions.

If Taking a Plane, Train, or Bus

Ask your travel agent or transportation representative to issue paperless tickets. These electronic versions waste less paper and can actually speed you through lines, since you won't have to purchase tickets at the airport.

Airlines are notorious for stuffing tickets, baggage receipts, and itineraries in paper jackets. In fact, a standard airline inside joke is that "every time a plane takes off a tree dies." Tell the counter clerks that you don't need the jackets.

When you get to the terminal or station at the other end, try using the hotel bus or van instead of renting a car. During your stay, relax and enjoy the scenery by leaving the driving to others or by taking public transportation. Even if you take a taxi, you'll keep an extra rental car off the road.

At the Hotel

Have towels and linens changed only every other day. Even then, make sure that towels and washcloths that haven't been used aren't replaced. Otherwise, perfectly clean items will be sent on a needlessly hot and sudsy tour of the laundry.

Turn off the heat or air conditioner when you leave the room. Make sure that the lights, water, television, and radio are off, too.

Take short, cooler showers.

Notify the housekeeping staff if the sink, shower, or toilet is leaking or dripping.

If you don't use one of the little amenity bottles in the bathroom, leave it for the next guest.

If traveling with children who need a little extra security, bring along a night-light instead of keeping the bathroom light blazing and fan whirring all night.

If the hotel has a brochure rack, take only the pamphlets you need.

If the hotel provides complimentary newspapers, pass your copy on to an associate or ask the hotel to recycle it when you're done reading.

Bring a plastic grocery bag from home for dirty laundry storage.

Turn off exercise equipment when finished. The same is true when done using the sauna, whirlpool, or Jacuzzi.

Still in the mood for a little exercise? Try the stairs rather than the elevator. (Just to be safe, first make sure the stairwells are well lit and that the doors are unlocked.)

Use the hotel's electronic check-out feature, if available. You can view your bill on the TV screen, approve it, and check out without any additional paperwork. Your credit-card statement will act as your receipt.

Many of the ideas listed above are practiced regularly by members of the "Green" Hotels Association. You can get their hotel membership list by calling (713) 789-8889 or by visiting their Web site at www.greenhotels.com.

Food

Try to avoid room service. Eating in your room means extra linens to be washed and extra energy used to keep your food warm. It also leads to excess food waste, since you will never use up all the ketchup and mustard in those cute little bottles, and the hotel will throw out any opened containers you leave behind.

Skip the minibar, also. Not only are products extravagantly expensive, but most are single serve, which means there's a lot of packaging and not a lot of product.

Take only a reasonable number of salt, pepper, sugar, ketchup, mustard, and mayonnaise packets.

Eat sit-down, rather than carry-out or fast-food, meals. There's much less packaging waste.

What to Do When Eating Out

If not overly hungry, try ordering two appetizers rather than a complete meal.

Many restaurants will serve half-portions and charge less. If you don't see this option on the menu, ask your server.

If you don't take cream in your coffee, mention this to your server before they bring the java to the table. This will cut down on the number of little cream containers that get tossed. Ditto for sugar.

You can reduce the number of jam, jelly, and butter packets that get thrown away either by not taking them, or by putting them aside on the table and pointing out to the busperson that you didn't use them.

If you bring leftovers home, remember to put them in the refrigerator right away. Also, put the doggie bag in the front of the fridge, where it can be seen and used quickly.

Help your children to order wisely. That old saying "My eyes were bigger than my stomach" is especially true when it comes to little ones.

Touring

Group tours are energy efficient. You get more people in fewer vehicles. If you're lucky, you'll make some new friends and save a little money, too.

Don't forget to bring your camera. Disposable cameras may be convenient, but they're wasteful.

Buy larger rolls of film. One roll of 36 creates 67 percent less waste than three rolls of 12 and costs much less, too. You'll probably save about 40 percent, or around $4.

If you plan on taking many indoor pictures, buy "fast" film that can be used without a flash or with a reduced flash, thus saving battery and bulb life. For reference, the ASA number on the film carton is an indication of film speed, with a higher number denoting faster film. Consider using ASA 400 or 800 film indoors, rather than ASA 100 or 200, which are better for outdoor lighting conditions.

If sending film through the mail for processing, write legibly. Kodak estimates that it receives 400,000 rolls of film each year that cannot be sent back to the owners, thanks to illegible handwriting.

As you can see, all our travel suggestions are pretty easy to do. Many will save you money, while all will help save resources. Bon voyage!

THE HOLIDAYS

Christ climbed down
from His bare Tree
this year
and ran away to where
no fat handshaking stranger
in a red flannel suit
and a fake white beard
went around . . .
bearing sacks of Humble Gifts
from Saks Fifth Avenue . . .
—Lawrence Ferlinghetti, "Christ Climbed Down"

Every year, between Thanksgiving and New Year's, the amount of trash we create increases by roughly 25 percent beyond what we normally discard during the rest of the year. This translates to an extra 5 million tons, or 10 billion pounds, of waste caused by our holiday eating, drinking, and gift giving habits. Don't get us wrong—we're very much in favor of warm and wonderful holidays. But we're also in favor of finding a few little things to do that will really reduce the environmental impact of Turkey Day, Hanukkah, Christmas, Kwanzaa, and New Year's Day—and, of course, the SUPERBOWL.

It's not hard to keep the holidays from going to your waste. And it's profitable, too. Looking down our list, pick a few of the things that make the most sense for you and your family. Once you get in the swing of things, you can try a few more ideas. Next thing you know, you'll be whistling "Green Christmas" as you enjoy the yearly festivities.

Portion Control

You've just finished your Thanksgiving dinner and left about a tablespoon of cranberry sauce on your plate and one little bite of turkey. Not much waste, right? Maybe not on *your* plate. But assuming we're alike, on our collective national plate it's an enormous waste—around 25 million pounds!

This example illustrates one of our biggest themes: *a little bit of effort from each of us can make an enormous difference.* We can't rely on a few stalwarts to do all the work. If each of us pitches in just a little, the results can be amazing.

Besides taking only as much food as you can eat, it's also a good idea for hosts and hostesses both to serve a little less, and maybe prepare a little less as well. Here are some portion guidelines to help you plan for meals and parties:

Portion Control, Holiday Style
(amount served per person)

Eggnog	$1/2$ cup
Cheese	2 oz.
Crackers	1–10
Celery	1 stalk
Turkey	$1/2$ lb. raw
Ham, roast beef	$1/3$ lb.
Squash, sweet potatoes	$1/2$ lb.
Broccoli, potatoes	$1/3$ lb.
Pie	$1/8$ pie

OTHER FOOD-RELATED TIPS

If buying a lot of soda, cut down on packaging by purchasing large-size bottles. If you insist on buying cans, forgo the cardboard boxes: they create over 90 percent more waste than the plastic rings.

Bread and cereal bags can be reused to store food and other items.

Send guests home with leftovers. Use paper and plastic bags and plastic containers. (This is a great way to get rid of all your excess bags and containers, as well as excess food.)

Buy potatoes and onions in plastic mesh bags. When tied in a big knot, the bags make terrific, long-lasting scouring pads.

Shopping and Gift Giving

Prepare a list of items ahead of time, so that you do less impulse shopping.

Plan trips in advance and consolidate so that you make fewer of them. Spending fewer hours driving to malls, shopping centers, and the post office means less wasted gas, time, and far less stress. *If we each saved one gallon of gas, the total amount of greenhouse gas emissions that would be prevented would total about 1 million tons.*

Shop early, while you have time to make careful choices. Last-minute spending often leads to panic buying, which leads to unwanted gifts. In fact, it's estimated that about *$4 billion worth of unwanted and unused gifts are purchased each year.*

Keep it simple—less can be more. One thoughtful gift may be more appreciated than six random items.

Shop at antique stores, holiday bazaars, and thrift shops. Someone's trash may very well be someone else's treasure.

Try shopping from home electronically. Use the phone, Internet, or TV to select, order, and send gifts.

Consolidate purchases into one bag. Better yet, bring along a few bags from home and reuse them.

Give gifts of yourself. Offer to baby-sit, wash the car, do the dishes, and other useful things.

Make your own gifts. For example, you can make wreaths out of natural materials such as branches, dried herbs, and red and green chilies. Wreath making is a great craft project for both children and adults.

Old items can make new gifts. How about using your creativity and your time to create a gift that will never be forgotten—or thrown out! A worn ironing board cover can be turned into new potholders and oven mitts. Empty lipstick cases make pretty, easy-to-find pillboxes. Used-up roll-on deodorant bottles can be refilled with poster paints for budding Picassos. And old clothes, drapes, and tablecloths can be used to make new doll clothes. Just use your imagination! In fact, create something full of yourself, such as a drawing or song, a poem, or a written remembrance of a special time. These are treasures for the recipient and for you—forever.

Since lots of toys need batteries, why not give rechargeable ones as a gift as well?

Donate unwanted gifts to charities, shelters, and the like.

Gift Wrap

Because it's coated, laminated, and embossed, gift wrap is not recyclable. Rather than buy it, why not use colorful, easily recycled paper you already have around the house, like the Sunday comics or an old subway map? Also, kids can use crayons or water-based paints to decorate paper bags for use as gift wrap— the kind parents and grandparents will cherish and want to keep, and maybe even frame.

Save fancier bags you received while shopping. Use them as gift bags or cut them up to make gift wrap.

Break down gift boxes and store them for next year. Those tins you've been saving in the pantry would make good boxes, too.

Reuse ribbon. If every family reused 2 feet of holiday ribbon, 38,000 miles' worth would be saved each year. That's enough to wrap a bow around the entire planet! (Don't forget that reusing ribbon also reduces the number of empty spools that have to be thrown away, too.)

Give gifts that don't need to be wrapped: tickets to concerts, museums, or sporting events; gift certificates; savings bonds; or donations to a favorite charity.

Rather than wrap oversize gifts, put a bow on them and hide them instead. Give the recipient clues to where the gift is hidden, turning the experience into a treasure hunt.

Make the wrap a useful part of the gift. Put cookies in a flowerpot or wrap a kitchen item in a colorful holiday-theme dish towel.

Shipping

Reuse packaging cartons and shipping materials. Old newspaper also makes for excellent packing. Bring home shredded paper from work and use that, too.

Drop off extra packaging materials such as peanuts and bubble wrap at local private mailing centers (e.g., Mail Boxes Etc.). Call the Plastic Loosefill Council (800-828-2214) for the names of local businesses that reuse them.

Paper grocery bags can be used to wrap and address small- to medium-size parcels for mailing.

Catalog Clutter and Junk Mail

In 1981, the typical family received 59 catalogs. By 1991, the number had jumped to 142. We don't know what it is today, but it's probably over 200. Here are a few strategies for eliminating much of the unwanted mail we receive virtually every day:

Call the 800 numbers printed on unwanted catalogs and ask to be removed from the list. Canceling ten catalogs will reduce your trash by 3.5 pounds per year (and make your postal carrier very happy!). If we all did this, the stack of canceled catalogs would be 2,000 miles high.

If you want to receive a catalog but think you're getting it too often, call and ask if they have a less frequent schedule. Many of the big national mailers, including Eddie Bauer, will change your schedule if you ask.

Reduce junk mail by calling the Mail Preference Service at (212) 768-7277 and ask for their free mail-reduction kit. Or you can write them at P.O. Box 9008, Farmingdale, NY 11735-9008.

Another, newer option is to write and ask to be removed from all of the direct marketing lists compiled by major credit bureaus. The "Big 3" are as follows:

Experian Opt-Out	**Equifax Options Trans**	**Union/ Transmark Inc.**
P.O. Box 919	P.O. Box 740123	555 W. Adams St.
Allen, TX 75013	Atlanta, GA 30374	Chicago, IL 60661
(800) 353-0809	(800) 755-3502	(800) 345-2349

If reducing unwanted mail is your thing, get a copy of *Stop Junk Mail Forever*. It's $3.95 and available from Good Advice Press, Box 78, Elizaville, NY 12523. Or call (914) 758-1400.

Cards

Each year, we send enough cards to fill a ten-story building the length and width of a football field. If we each sent just one fewer card, the volume of trash would be reduced by one full story, or 450,000 cubic feet. Here's what to do:

Be selective when you send cards. If you haven't heard from someone in a few years, don't send them a card. You'll save money and the resources and energy involved in their manufacture and transport.

Send holiday postcards. Both postage and paper are reduced.

If you have leftover cards from years gone by that haven't been used, send them to the new people on your list. They won't know the difference.

Cut off the front of cards you receive and reuse them as postcards, gift cards, or ornaments. Recycle the rest, along with the envelopes.

Send the fronts of cards to St. Jude's Ranch for Children, and they'll be recycled into new cards. The address is 100 St. Jude's St., Boulder City, NV 89005-1618. You can also buy reused/recycled cards from them. Call (800) 492-3562. A packet of ten cards costs $6.50.

Make sure you have addressed cards correctly and legibly. The post office estimates that up to 20 percent of mail is incorrectly addressed, making it undeliverable and thus completely wasted.

For business associates, e-mail or a phone call will often do. Hearing from you via computer or phone can be just as personal or friendly as a note in the mail.

Decking the Halls

You can make your home look festive and friendly without spending a fortune or generating lots of waste. For example:

Buy a tree that can be planted or mulched. Artificial ones also reduce the number of trees that need to be grown and harvested. (For reference, 50 million Christmas trees are purchased each year in the United States!)

Make your own wreaths and garlands, using dried flowers, branches, pine cones, and the like. Much of this material is available for the taking, right in your back yard.

Put all your Christmas lights on timers. You'll save energy and also make your house seem lived in while you're away.

Buy strands of lights that are wired in parallel, rather than series. If one bulb goes out, the others still work. This makes replacing bulbs much easier and reduces the temptation to throw away "bad" strands. *Hint:* Parallel strands are usually long and straight, with a plug at one end and a receptacle at the other. Bulbs wired in series generally come in loops, with only a plug.

Use smaller, lower wattage bulbs. They consume less electricity and give off less heat—a definite safety plus around the tree.

When taking lights off the tree or house, keep them

untangled by wrapping them around some rolled-up newspaper. You can also use the cardboard core from a roll of wrapping paper, keeping it out of the trash and extending its useful life.

Party Time

Going to a party? Walk if it's close, or carpool with friends. If bringing a "hostess gift," check to see if you already have a bottle of wine on hand or box of candy that can be used for the occasion. (Just make sure the party givers weren't the ones who gave the item to you!)

Giving a party? Turn the thermostat down before the guests arrive. Their extra body heat will warm the room.

Send guests home with goody bags filled with leftovers.

Need formal wear? Consider renting, rather than buying, a gown or tuxedo. If you feel the need to buy, try a thrift shop first. You'd be amazed at the number of originally expensive dresses and suits that are hanging on their racks.

Throw a White Elephant party at home, work, or church a few days after Christmas. Ask friends and co-workers to bring in two unwanted items, unwrapped. Then you can either draw numbers and pick gifts or auction the items off, donating the money to a good cause. In either case, you'll be amazed at how quickly all of these previously un-wanted items find useful lives in new homes.

'Twas the Night Before Christmas

Hint to children: Don't put out too much food for Santa and his reindeer. Maybe a cookie or two, or a few carrots. You might want to ask Mom or Dad what each of them would eat late at night, and assume that Santa would want the same.

CONCLUSIONS

We have seen the enemy . . .
—Walt Kelly, *Pogo*

After reading this far, it should be obvious that the long-term health of both our society and the environment requires that we start reducing consumption of resources, as well as working to minimize waste and garbage. So what's stopping us?

First, as we discussed in an early chapter of this book, there is all of our hunter-gather preprogramming that conditions us to adopt simple black-and-white solutions to problems, but only when these difficulties are staring us in the face.

Second, and just as basic to our human nature, are the powerful forces over the last 2 million years that have encouraged us to consume. Literally, ever since we were

identifiable as hominids—the first humanlike creatures—
we had material stuff. In fact, the first humanlike creatures
were identified as such because of the litter from making
stone tools and the tools themselves that were left behind.

The reason that we are so intimately associated with
material goods is that they are critical to our becoming
more than just survivors. What we could invent, produce,
and use made the difference between whether or not we
prospered as a species. In this manner, stuff became a
critical component in a most vicious cycle. The more we
prospered by using the tools we made, the more we in-
vented, made, and used more tools.

If that weren't enough of a material monkey on our
back, we began to think abstractly and use language. Ironically, making and using tools played an important role in
the development of both new skills. In fact, right along
with our new skills came great bunches of new stuff to
symbolize all the abstract things we were thinking and now
talking about—like cave paintings showing us hunting for
food; Venus figurines symbolizing religion and fertility;
and elaborate displays of wealth to indicate our status both
before and after our deaths. Status goods, in fact, provided
an exponential leap in the amount of stuff we produced
and admired because they could be made as separate
items (necklaces or bracelets) or they could be added onto
basic tools (like brand names on hand tools, purses, or
blue jeans).

Even language became so totally enmeshed in stuff that
it literally became stuff itself! Writing always has to be on

something (from clay tablets to acid-free archival paper) and written by something (from pencil lead to laser-printer inks). How much more inextricably involved can you get? We use written stuff to teach language, to record legal language and all legal statements, to enrich our minds, to entertain ourselves, to advertise ourselves and our stuff, and *even to tell ourselves how to use less of it!* (Let's hope, in this case, a little more stuff in the form of this book will ultimately equal less.)

But don't despair! We realize that material goods were critically important to our ancestors in the past and are equally important in defining who we are today. That's why we're not asking for abstinence, but only for a little forbearance—whatever little you can do. And if everyone does a little, it will actually add up to quite a lot!

Take one example—one that is not the highest on our agenda, but nevertheless is important to preserving the environment: decreasing the consumption of meat. As we stated previously, consuming meat is a very inefficient way to provide our bodies with nutrients. It would be far more efficient, and probably more healthy, if we placed greater emphasis on increasing our intake of fruits, grains, and vegetables for much of our nutritional and dietetic needs.

Reducing meat use slightly is something we can all do without too much bother. In fact, *each of us doing a little in this regard is better than having a few people do it all.* Think about the 12.5 million out of 270 million Americans who are vegetarians. By not eating meat, this 5 percent of the population saves significant resources, since beef, pork, and lamb production of protein and other nutrients can be ten times as energy intensive as vegetable production. (Never mind the significant amount of methane-related air pollution created by those cows, pigs, and sheep!)

But this "5 percent solution" can do *no more* than reduce consumption by the same 5 percent. In contrast, if the other 95 percent of the population stops eating meat for just one day a week, the result would be a 14 percent decrease in its consumption. Thus, we will achieve almost three times the overall savings for 86 percent less individual effort. And certainly, going without meat one day a week is hardly a sacrifice. In fact, it's easy to imagine a weekly savings of $3 at the grocery store, or $156 per year. Not bad for one little change.

The same is true of the following:

Driving your car. If everyone drove one day less per month and saved 2 gallons of gasoline each time, we'd reduce total annual gasoline consumption by 1.5 billion gallons and carbon dioxide production by 16.5 million tons. (We would also save about $30 each!)

Food waste. If every single one of us wasted one less ounce of food per week, it would reduce annual food waste by 750 million pounds.

Packaging waste. Reducing packaging waste by 1 pound per month per family would cut packaging discards by 1.2 billion pounds, or 6 million tons.

Paper waste. Using one less sheet of paper per day at your office cuts your personal consumption by half a ream, or 250 sheets, per year. That's about 5 pounds you've saved. In a typical company with 1,000 employees, that equals 2.5 tons of paper that isn't used—saving trees, water, and energy while reducing pollution and green-house gas emissions.

We're not saying that you should do everything we suggest. But please do *something*. For starters, pick things that save you the most money. Just remember that every time you save financial resources, we all save natural resources. That's a win-win situation that's as easy on the planet as it is on your wallet.

It is also a win-win situation for our civilization. If everyone would decide to follow just a few suggestions, then the results would be visible—IMMEDIATELY!

This is a new kind of environmentalism, what we call *environmentalism for who we really are.* If we listen to it and take it seriously, it is the best way for us to become the first culture in the history of the world to learn to use less stuff—in time to continue to survive where others have collapsed.

As we said in the introduction, what we're talking about here is a war on waste. It's a war that humanity, through its voracious consumption of resources, has been responsible for creating and must be responsible for ending.

Like all wars, winning this one will require a tremen-dous understanding of human nature and the judicious use, as well as conservation, of scarce resources. But, unlike other wars, our objective is not to kill our enemies, but to save them. For as Pogo said, *"We have seen the enemy, and they is us."*

And how do we save ourselves? We use less stuff!

APPENDIX

In researching and preparing this book, the following sources were used:

Allman, William F. *The Stone Age Present*. New York: Touchstone Books, 1995.

Bailey, Ronald. *The True State of the Planet*. New York: Simon and Schuster, 1995.

Ball, Jeff, and Liz Ball. *Smart Yard*. Golden, Colo.: Fulcrum, 1996.

Ball, Jeff, and Robert Kourik. *Easy Composting*. San Ramon, Calif.: Ortho Books, 1992.

Basic Plumbing Illustrated. 3rd ed. Menlo Park, Calif.: Sunset Publishing, October 1992.

Berlin, Brent, and Paul Kay. *Basic Color Terms: Their Universality and Evolution*. Berkeley: University of California Press, 1969.

Bradley, Fern Marshall, ed. *Garden Answers*. Emmaus, Penn.: Rodale Press, 1995.

Cherson, Peter. Personal communication, August 28, 1990.

City Public Service, San Antonio, Texas.

Consumer Reports, April 1991.

Credit Counseling Services of New York, Inc., Farmingdale, New York.

Dawkins, Richard. *The Selfish Gene.* New York: Oxford University Press, 1976.

Dobyns, Susan, and Wilson W. Hughes. *WRAP Service Manual.* The Garbage Project, University of Arizona, Tucson, 1994.

"End of the Road for Carpooling." *USA Today,* January 28, 1998.

Environmental Protection Agency. *Characterization of Municipal Solid Waste in the United States.* Washington, D.C.: EPA, 1996.

Federal Reserve Board, Washington, D.C.

Gibson, McGuire. "Violation of Fallow and Engineered Disaster in Mesopotamian Civilization." In *Irrigation's Impact on Society,* ed. Ted Downing and McGuire Gibson, pp. 7–19. Tucson: University of Arizona Press, 1974.

Harrison, Gail G., M. L. Mapes, and William Rathje. "Trash Tells a Tale: Studies of School Food Waste in Nutrition Education." *Illinois Teacher,* May/June 1976, pp. 298–304.

Heath, et al. *Applications of Heuristics and Biases in Social Issues.* New York: Plenum Press, 1994.

Jacobsen, Thorkild, and R. McC. Adams. "Salt and Silt in Ancient Mesopotamian Agriculture." *Science* 128 (1958): 1251–58.

Kay, Jane Holtz. *Asphalt Nation.* New York: Random House, 1997.

Leakey, Richard, and Roger Lewen. *The Sixth Extinction.* New York: Doubleday, 1995.

Lewis, Tom. *Divided Highway.* New York: Viking Penguin, 1997.

Lippa, Richard A. *Introduction to Social Psychology.* Pacific Grove, Calif.: Brooks/Cole, 1994.

Marker, Rom J. *The Supermarket: An Analysis of Growth,*

Development, and Change. Pullman, Wash.: Washington State University Press, 1963.

Narducci, Patty. "The Effects of 'Offer vs. Serve' on Plate Waste in Elementary Schools in Tucson." Master's thesis, University of Arizona, Tucson, 1986.

The New Student Color Set. New York: Fairchild Books, 1997.

Poundstone, William. *Prisoner's Dilemma.* New York: Anchor, 1992.

Progressive Grocer. 1996 Marketing Guidebook and Competitive Edge, May 1996.

Rathje, William. "In Praise of Archaeology: Le Projet du Garbage." In *Historic Archaeology and the Importance of Material Things,* ed. Leland Ferguson, pp. 36–42. Society for Historical Archaeology, 1977.

Rathje, William, and Cullen Murphy. *Rubbish! The Archaeology of Contemporary Garbage.* New York: HarperCollins, 1991.

Rathje, W. L. "Classic Maya Development and Denouement." In *The Classic Maya Collapse,* ed. T. P. Culbert. Albuquerque, N.M.: University of New Mexico Press, 1973.

Reber, Arthur S. *Dictionary of Psychology,* 2d ed. New York: Penguin, 1995.

Rogers, Everett M. *Diffusion of Innovations.* New York: Free Press and Macmillan, 1983.

Schele, Linda, and David Freidel. *A Forest of Kings: The Untold Story of the Ancient Maya.* New York: Morrow, 1990.

Schwing, R., and W. A. Albers Jr., eds. *Societal Risk Assessment: How Safe Is Safe Enough?* New York: Plenum Press, 1980.

Sempe, Peter M. *The Fifth Discipline.* New York: Doubleday/Currency, 1990.

Shankle, Susan. *The Joy of Carpooling.* San Mateo, Calif.: self-published, 1994.

Supermarkets: 50 Years of Progress. Washington, D.C.: Food Marketing Institute, 1980.

ULS Report, July–August 1997.

Waldfogel, Joel. "The Deadweight Loss of Christmas." *American Economic Review,* December 1993.

Wheat, Joe Ben. *The Olsen-Chubbock Site: A Paleo-Indian Bison Kill.* Washington, D.C.: Smithsonian Institution and the Society for American Archaeology, 1972.

INDEX

ABOUT THE
AUTHORS

Robert Lilienfeld is editor of *The ULS (Use Less Stuff) Report*, a highly respected and widely read newsletter aimed at spreading the benefits of conservation and waste prevention. He is also president of the Cygnus Group, an Ann Arbor–based consulting firm working with progressive businesses in the area of sustainable development, and serves as an Advisory Board member for the University of Michigan's Corporate Environmental Management Program (CEMP). He is interviewed regularly on environmental issues by a wide variety of national, regional, and local media outlets, and has his own monthly commentary on public radio.

As a professor of anthropology at the University of Arizona and the founder/director of the Garbage Project, **Dr. William Rathje** is known as the nation's "garbologist"— the man who taught Americans about their consumption habits by rummaging through their garbage. Dr. Rathje co-authored the bestseller *Rubbish!* with *Atlantic Monthly* managing editor Cullen Murphy. He is also a regular contributor to *The ULS Report* and a variety of other publications.